PRACTICES AND CHALLENGES OF INCLUSIVE EDUCATION WITH DISABILTIES

PRACTICES AND CHALLENGES OF INCLUSIVE EDUCATION WITH DISABILTIES

Dr. Karanam Viswa Bhushan

GYAN

Published, 2021

Published by

Gyan Publishing House
5, Ansari Road
Daryaganj, New Delhi-110002
Phone: 011-47034999, 9811692060
www.gyanbooks.com
E-mail: books@gyanbooks.com

Printed at: Gyan Press, Delhi.

Cataloging in Publication Data—DK
Courtesy: D.K. Agencies (P) Ltd. <docinfo@dkagencies.com>

Bhushan, Karanam Viswa, 1963- **author.**
Practices and challenges of early education with disabilities / Dr. Karanam Viswa Bhushan.
pages cm
Includes bibliographical references and index.
ISBN 9788121220323 (HB)

1. Children with disabilities—Education (Early childhood)—Ethiopia. 2. Inclusive education—Ethiopia. I. Title.

LCC LC4019.3.B48 2021 | DDC 371.90472 23

Contents

Acknowledgements

I would like to thank and express my special glory to the Almighty God.

I would like to express my gratitude to my student Meskerem Dalata and a number of individuals and institutions who supported.

I would like to express my in-depth appreciation and gratitude to Gambella Town Administration Education Office workers in all and the head of the education office and special needs education expert in particular for their valuable collaboration and support.

I also like to thank all teachers, school principals, cluster supervisors, students including disability and different institutions who cooperated and participated in the giving the necessary information needed to the research.

I would like to extend my heartfelt thanks to my friend Ria Vinkx who has invisible support through her wishes and blessings in all my works.

List of Tables

List of Figures

Abbreviations

ADA	: American Disability Act
APA	: American Psychiatric Association
CSN	: Children Special Needs
CWDs	: Children with Disabilities
DBSTs	: District-Based Support Teams
ESDP IV & V	: Educational Strategic Development Program Four and Five
ETP	: Education and Training Policy
EFA	: Education for All
GTP	: Growths and Transformation Plan
IE	: Inclusive Education
ILO	: International Labour Organisation
MOE	: Ministry of Education
PTA	: Parent Teacher Association
PWD	: People with Disabilities
SBST	: School-Based Support Team
SNE	: Special Needs Education
SWD	: Student with Disabilities
SWSEN	: Students with Special Education Needs
UNDP	: United Nations Development Programme
UNESCO	: United Nations Educational, Scientific and Cultural Organisation
UNFPA	: United Nations Population Fund Activities
UN	: United Nations

UPIAS	: Union of Physically Impaired Against Segregation
WHO	: World Health Organisation
WP6	: White Paper 6 on Special Needs Education: Building an Inclusive Education and Training System

Chapter One
Introduction

1.1 Background of the Study

Inclusive education is a global agenda; it means the complete inclusion in all aspects of schooling of children of different abilities that other children have the ability to access. Teachers were seen as key people and considered to play an important role in bringing about such educational change. According to the American Psychological Association (APA), terms such as special educational needs applies to the need for persons with sensory disabilities, speech disorders, learning difficulties, motor skill illnesses, behavioural problems and mental retardation disorders (Ehsaan & Shahid, 2016).

Education is civilisation's transmission. But when this writer asked if they believed that the transmission of civilisation could be regarded as a kind of education with the aid of war, no one answered and the discussion was cut short. *"Education is the socially organised and regulated process of continuous transference of socially significant experience from the previous generations to the followings. The main way to receive an education is to take a course of training in the system of educational institutions."* Education was the method of transmitting and receiving according to the concept (Reviews, Reports, & Parent, 2017).

Inclusive education is an approach to combining in school environments with special education and general education students to promote diversity, lifelong learning, and create a more equitable society. An overview of inclusive education practices will educate stakeholders about the state of inclusive learning, identify the situational factors that affect programme implementation and suggest concrete start-up or improvement measures for inclusive education programmes (Tahir *et al,* 2019).

The practice of inclusive education receives an increasing number of strong in improvements additional support and interest in education system in almost all countries in the world. There is a definitely declared agreement in the world that all children have the right to education regardless of their race, gender, nationality, incapacity etc. And these agreements have been indicated in generally important documents. Inclusive education may be a method of strengthening the capability of the education system to achieve resolute all learners and might therefore be understood as a key strategy to realise education for all (EFA). The history of inclusive education times back to the Universal Declaration of Human Rights (1948) that emphasises that everybody has the proper to education. Moreover, the quality Rules on the exploit of Opportunities for Persons with Disabilities (1993) emphasised rights of education children with special needs. Another globally important agreement supporting CSN is world organisation Convention on the Rights of Persons with Disabilities (Suleymanov, 2015).

According to (McLaren, 2013) although, inclusion is also useful for several students, students with disorder posture specific challenges and exclusions within the inclusive possibility. Extremely advanced behavioural, social, and educational needs attended with sensory process difficulties will build inclusion difficult.

Although, Parekh (2013) described that, In closely every country, inclusive education has emerged as one of SWSEN [Students with Special Education Needs]'s most dominant issues. The area of special needs education has evolved over the last 40 years from a model of apartheid by incorporation to a stage where diversity is integral to public discussion.

The most agenda for this conference was Education for exhausted the entire world. Inclusive education is presently a topical subject that's wide mentioned and debated upon within the field of education, African nation bounded. It's invariably been cited as a part of the worldwide education for all agenda as a replacement education model and as an academic reform goals to create our societies inclusive. Identical is accepted in Tanzania; but the side of education for all isn't effectively enforced despite of getting policies and legal framework that advocate education for all (Udoba, 2014).

According to UNESCO (2009) as cited in Sikandar (2017), Sixty seven million children of ability grade school, grammar school and elementary school age area unit out of ability's; of that one-third sleep in South Asia and Sub-Saharan Africa wherever children with Disabilities (CWDs) create one-third out of school children.

The current state of education in South Africa can be traced in part to the legacy of apartheid education policies. (Engelbrecht, 2006) argues that the central feature that distinguishes South Africa from other countries in terms of education is the degree to which racially ingrained attitudes and the institutionalisation of discriminatory practices have resulted in significant inequalities in education provision, a consequence of the division and injustice that defined society as a whole (Safford *et al*, 2018).

Education is a human right for all. As indicated in Article 26 of the 1948 Human Rights Declaration education as a right is stated as; "everyone has the right to education." In this regard, education as a right for all is acknowledged as education shall be free, at least in the elementary and fundamental stages; in addition, it affirmed that elementary education shall be compulsory and it shall be intended for the full advancement of the human personality and to the strengthening of respect for human rights and fundamental freedoms (UN, 1948).

In addition, Ethiopian person with disability organisation (2005), as cited in (Mitiku, 2014). Inclusive education means that welcoming all children, while not discrimination into regular or general schools. By the modification of perspective against differential treatment of education variations in individuals can probably be seen in a very positive perspective.

Ethiopia has designed and implemented various legal frameworks that can support the effectiveness of access and quality of inclusive education for children with disability. Even though Ethiopia has accepted various international conventions and policy instruments the participation rate of children with disabilities (CWDs) still insignificant and did not achieve the needs of children with disabilities as well as for those of with special talents (Sori, Azale, & Gemeda, 2016).

In addition, ESDP five of MoE (2015), indicated that the exact number of disabled children in Ethiopia is unknown. Instead the WHO estimate rate is used for planning purposes, stating that the prevalence of disabled people in any population will 10 million.

Therefore, people with disabilities had a convincing role in taking part in the scholastic journey in the history of Ethiopian church learning. For this, during his visit to Ethiopia in the early 16th century, Francisco Alvarez gave his evidence. During the Portuguese visit to Ethiopia in the 1520s, Alvarez mentioned his surprise at seeing the inclusion of persons with disabilities in the ranks of the Ethiopian priesthood (Alvarez, 1 AD).

In the earlier times, when the life and work of Ethiopian society was dominated by Christian faith, the education of people with visual and physical disabilities, as well as those with talent and ability (Zalalem Temesgen, 2014). In general, inclusive education is making good accessibility of general education to students those who are student with disability and not with out of marginalisation of each other in school. It mean that including children in learning as equal to healthy ones.

1.2 Statement of the Problem

This study was designed to assess the practices and challenges of inclusive education for children with disabilities in primary schools of Gambella Town. As indicated in Education Sector Development Programme four (MOE, 2010), inclusive education is a process of addressing and responding to the diversity of needs of all earners through increasing participation and reducing exclusion within and from education.

In average, 10% of any population is disabled. With this assumption approximately 85% of the world's children with disability of the age below 15 years live in the developing countries. The right to education for all children is protected in the universal declaration of human rights. However, in developing countries, the proportion of disabled children attending school is estimated between less than 1% and 5% (Esther & Aluko, 2014).

Inclusive education as a process to address and respond to the heterogeneity of needs of all children, youth and adults by increasing inclusion, cultures and societies, and by reducing and denying exclusion within and from the education system. This implies that we are talking not only to mentally or physically abused students, as well as to all students with special educational needs which may hamper their performance in school (UNESCO, 2009).

According to (Megan, 2017), as suggested in his study on Inclusion of Students with Special Needs in the General Education Classroom has been a major topic of discussion for many years. Inclusion education means that all pupils, regardless of their strengths and weaknesses, are part of the school family. There is no need to place students with disabilities in different institutions. We earn full access to all the resources and social interactions available in the classroom in general education. The presence of students with disabilities in the general education classroom is an existing legal provision in the United States according to the special education legislation of the country known as Individuals with Disabilities Education Act.

Education support services are under-resourced and unable to address the large number of needy students their learning barriers are not addressed. School teachers are supposed to support students experiencing learning barriers, but they do not seem to have the skills and knowledge to do so. SBSTs and District-Based Support Teams (DBSTs) should be responsible for empowering teachers to address barriers to learning, according to WP6 (White Paper 6 on Special Needs Education: Building an Inclusive Education and Training System). Hence, investigating teacher help in addressing and reducing obstacles to education, particularly in primary school, was considered important (Matlala, 2015).

Even though, Pingle and Garg (2015) conducted their study on Effect of Inclusive Education Awareness System on Pre-service Teachers and had got their finding of the innovative community conservation educators have achieved diffident understanding of inclusive learning. There was no major interpersonal age, socio-economic status, social intelligence, emotional intelligence, and treatment impact. It indicates the efficacy of the treatment given to the experimental group. Furthermore, when government and various scholars have conducted various studies and assessments to improve both access and quality of IE for CWDs, there is still a problem with access to quality education for CWDs. Consequently, despite the fact that several attempts were made to evaluate challenges going through the implementation of IE for CWDs each at international and country stages, maximum of them have been targeted on policy, economic, school and socio-cultural factors not on personal elements within children with disabilities and most of the research have been undertaken at higher stage and actual.

According to (Mitiku, Alemu, and Mengsitu, 2014), conducted their study on challenges and opportunity to implement inclusive Education in North Gondar zone by using descriptive survey research design. The Study shows that, while there are some opportunities to support inclusive education, due to lack of awareness, commitment and collaboration, it cannot be taken as a guarantee. And there are real challenges that prevent inclusive education from being fully implemented. Overall, the definition and realistic change must be applicable in Ethiopian schools as our country is not free from the practice of educational exclusion, especially for people with disabilities, so this study, assess the challenges and opportunities of providing inclusive education in our school system to evaluate the challenges and opportunities for inclusive education in North Gondar Zone's chosen primary schools.

Challenges and opportunities in Inclusion of Students with Physical Disabilities in Physical Education Practical Classes in the case of Secondary Schools of North Shewa Zone. He got finding through mixed research approach. Findings of the study shows that, lack of support and encouragement from teachers in practical classes for students with disabilities; inadequate training and poor experience of physical education teachers; lack of relevant curriculum materials for SWD, such as textbooks, teachers' guides, etc.; lack of professional support from Worde and Zone Education Officers to schools to promote inclusiveness (Kassaw, 2017).

According to UNESCO (2015), concerned to despite the fact that various studies and the assessments had been conducted by government and unique learners to enhance each the get entry to and great of IE for CWDs, there is still a problem on having access to pleasant education to CWDs in number one abilities of Ethiopia. From my experience, inclusive education in Gambella town it is not a new approach compared to the other regions of Ethiopia. But the practice of inclusive education is poor in case of low attention of local government especially education sector and bodies concerned in fulfilling educational infrastructures for children disability like brail, especial teachers of children with disability, buildings and low attitude of community toward those students to attend the school is also challenging. This all motivated the researcher to conduct the study in the study area. The purpose of this study is to identify the practices of inclusive education and challenges that in Gambella town through assessment and provides recommendation depending on the finding of the study. The study will fill the above mentioned gap through identifying good and weak practices of inclusive education and also challenges that affect the effectiveness of the practices and recommend to continue the good and to solve their weakness. After this study, the audience will get some knowledge from it what does inclusive education mean, what are the practices and challenges just like in the world, Africa and Ethiopia in general and in Gambella in particular. It will be clearly shows the current status of inclusive education in Gambella town. The challenges will be solved by the bodies concerned depending on the recommendation. On the other hand, the study will be used as input for educational sectors and bodies concerned for decision-making and also reference for other researchers. Therefore, even though several attempts have been made to assess challenges facing the implementation of IE for CWDs both at world and country levels, most of them were focused on policy, economic, school and socio-cultural factors not on personal factors within children with disabilities and most of the studies were undertaken at higher level and urban not at grass root/ school level and marginalised regions like Gambella Regional State. In addition, even if various studies and the assessments were conducted by government and different scholars to improve both the access and quality of IE for CWDs, there is still a problem on accessing quality education to CWDs in primary schools of Ethiopia particularly in the study area. Based on this, here the study has been tried to assess the practices and challenges of IE for CWDs in primary schools of Gambella Town which is located in one of marginalised regions Gambell a regional state. Therefore, this study was under taken at school level tried to investigate personal factors in addition to school, socio-cultural and economic factors influencing the implementation of IE. Here, the findings of this study in turn would help in improving the application of inclusive education that would have make schools attractive and comfortable to all children equally.

In addition to the practical problems which the study area faced, no systematic study has been conducted to address the issues in this particular area to come up with a solution to reverse the situation. In this regard, this study desired to assess the practice of inclusive education for students with disabilities, the role of local government in implementing inclusive education and challenges facing to implement inclusive education initiatives in study area.

1.3 Basic Research Questions

This study investigates the practical implementation and challenges that are hindering the effectiveness of inclusive education for children with disabilities by focusing on the access and quality of the programme in the study area by searching answers for the following basic research questions:

1. What is the practice of inclusive education for all students in Gambella town?
2. What is the role of local government in implementing inclusive education in study area?
3. What are the challenges facing to implement inclusive education for all in study area?

1.4 Objectives of the Study

1.4.1 General Objective of the Study

The overall objective of this study is to assess the practices and challenges of inclusive education for children with disabilities in primary schools of Gambella town.

1.4.2 Specific Objectives of the Study

The study has the following specific objectives:-

1. To assess the practice of inclusive education for students with disabilities in study area.

2. To assess the role of local government in implementing inclusive education in study area.

3. To identify the challenges facing to implement inclusive education initiatives in study area.

1.5 The Scope of the Study

The study were undertaken to investigate the practice and challenges of inclusive education for all students/ including with disability students in Gambella town administration primary school. The study used to focus on inclusive education for all students. The study was conducted through mixed research approach with cross-sectional survey on 2019/2020 academic year. The data were starting to collect from February 2020 up to March 2020 G.C. from the respondents of the study area. These studies were defined to verify the realistic implementation and challenges of inclusive education for children with disabilities primary schools in Gambella town administration. The crucial size of observable surrounded to the general practices and boundaries associated with socio-cultural, school, economic and private elements that restrict the implementation of inclusive education for children with disabilities each in terms of registration and enjoyable.

1.6 Significance of the Study

Understanding the practice and challenges of IE with disabilities used to help in planning intervention. Although study is conducted primarily as an academic requirement it provides feedback on current practices and challenges in the implementation of inclusive education in Gambella town administration to educational leader's teachers, students and other stakeholders. The study is significant for it increases individuals considerate concerning the practices and challenges of inclusive education on primary school. Since regular schools should be inclusive in order that all children will learn along, wherever potential, however any difficulties or variations they will have. Therefore, in order to deal with numerous desires of these students particularly the wants of children with disabilities the education system should be able to answer this numerous desires of children each quantifiable and mental setup. Therefore, this study will likely to feature additional info to the fundamental knowledge on the practices and challenges facing inclusive education for children with disabilities. It's significant for it increases individuals considerate concerning the problems that influence practices and challenges of inclusive education on primary school. Since regular schools have to be inclusive in order that all children will learn along, anywhere capacity, nevertheless any difficulties or variations they'll have. Therefore, in order to address numerous desires of those students particularly the needs of children with disabilities the education system need to be capable of answer this numerous desires of children each quantifiable and mental setup. Consequently, this observe will be in all likelihood to characteristic extra information to the fundamental understanding at the practices and challenges facing inclusive education for children with disabilities. The findings will possibly have truly indicated the modern-day-day practices and essential difficult conditions for the transport of inclusive education.

1.7 Organisation of the Thesis

This paper will be organised in five chapters. Chapter one deals with the background of the study, statement of the problem, basic research question, objectives of the study, significance of the study, scope of the study, Limitation of the study and definition of relevant concepts for the study. Chapter two is devoted to the review of related literature, the theoretical and empirical review of practice and challenges of inclusive education on primary school. It reviewed literature on the practice and challenges of inclusive education and how other Ethiopian countries relate to the concept. Chapter three handles the research methodology and model specification. In this chapter the description of the study area, the sources of data, and the methods used to obtain the data and the theoretical and econometric models used for analyzing the data set are presented. It offers an explanation on the framework on how data was gathered as well as the sampling procedure used in this study and Chapter four will focus on data presentation, analysis and interpretation. It presents and analyses of the findings on practice and challenges of inclusive education in Gambella town administration. Finally, Chapter five will present the findings of the study, draws the conclusion and makes recommendations based on the findings of the study.

1.8 Limitation of the Study

While the researcher has conducted the study, there were some constraints faced. These include Coved-19 corona virus problems and some respondents' repelled to return the questionnaire. In addition, this study was not addressed all primary schools in the Town, the Region and Ethiopia in broad because of financial problem.

Chapter Two

Literature Review

2.1 Introduction

This chapter will focused on examining concepts, theories and the findings of different relative considers which were conducted by utilising other analysts on inclusive education both locally and over the world. Hence, the elemental concepts and speculations and the experiences on the given issue are assessed and analyzed in arrange to clarify the issue which is intended for investigating its practices and challenges in primary schools of the given location.

2.2 Basic Concept of Inclusive Education

(Ahsan,M.T., 2013) in his article 'Inclusive Education for Children with Special Needs in Bangladesh' stated that 'Bangladesh is not behind other developed countries in enacting laws and declarations in favours of inclusive education, but lack of resources is the main barrier to the implementation of inclusive education'. He also mentioned that 'in developed countries such as Australia, virtually all school-age children with disabilities are in education, while in Bangladesh, 89 percent of children with disabilities are not in education.' He also proposed several additional initiatives to improve IE in Bangladesh, such as connecting programmes between regular and special schools, arrangements for dual placement, development of special units in regular schools, initiation of model schools for others to follow and inter-ministerial and inter-agency partnerships to improve inclusive education practices.

2.3 Definition of Key Terms

In short the definition of key terms used in exploring the practice and challenges of inclusive education for children with disabilities.

A. Inclusive Education: The term inclusive education used in this textbook considers the understanding of inclusion as an approach to all children's education. Human rights to education are at the heart of inclusive education (University of Minnesota, 2019). Inclusive education is a form of education in which individuals with learning disabilities are emotionally invested in the normal classroom environment, resulting in alterations in attitudes, curricula, and environments to meet all learners ' needs. 'Inclusive education' has come to be a commonly used buzz phrase.

Inclusive education as eliminating what excludes and marginalises means that education is not just about making schools accessible to those who are already in a position to access them; instead, the goal of inclusive education is to identify and remove barriers to inclusion in education. Inclusive education is therefore about being involved in finding obstacles and barriers that learners face about trying to access resources for quality education, as well as removing barriers and barriers that contribute to exclusion (UNESCO, 2012).

Each child has the right to education. This includes disabled children. The CRPD goes further to stress that inclusive education for every child with a disability is a fundamental human right. An inclusive education system is one that accommodates all students at all levels–pre-school, primary, secondary, tertiary, technical, and lifelong learning, irrespective of their abilities or requirements (UNICEF, 2017).

B. Challenges: The use of the term challenges in this study refers to factors that make inclusive education uncertain and that make it difficult for learners to deal with effectively and with difficulty. This reflects the conditions that put significant demands on educators who are the key implementers of inclusive education.

C. Disabilities: Disability is a set of social restrictions and constraints on the pursuit of full and equal participation by persons with disabilities. Within the case of the medical adaptation, the focus of the definition is on the physical and mental challenges of the individual in differentiate with what is regarded as normal physical and mental status. But within the case of at that point social demonstrate it appears into a whole extend of physical and social environment which will be balanced in a way that would help the individual with functional impediments to discharge his/her capacity in full (Howgego, Miles, & Myers, 2014).

Disability is one of the most ignored sources of academic failure and among those exempted from schools, children with disabilities are disproportionately represented (Murungi, 2015). In Malawi and the United Republic of Tanzania, having a disability increases the probability of never attending school and in Burkina Faso; there is a two-fold increase in the risk of children out of school. The concept of Disabilities is characterised in an unexpected way based on different point of view and objective.

In each race, ethnicity, class, sexual orientation, age, and religion, disability is present. More than a billion people have some form of illness, nearly 15 percent of the world's population. Of these, an estimated 150 million children are disabled and 80% live in the developing world (World Health Organisation [WHO], 2011).

According to (Secretariat of the African Decade of Persons with Disabilities, 2010) explain that, the concept of disability is defined differently based on different perspective and intention. The definition of disability has evolved from what is known as an individual focused (medical model) definition to the environment focused (social model) definition.

As defined by WHO (1980), disability is any restriction or lack (resulting from impairment) of ability to perform an activity in the manner or within the range considered as normal for human beings. Disability as, a state in which functional limitations and/or impairments are factors of existing difficulties in performing one or more activities which, (in accordance with the subjects' age, sex and normative social role) generally accepted as essential basic components of daily living such as self-care, social relationship and economic activity (ILO, 2006).

D. Inclusion: *"Inclusion is the process through which learners, particularly those with learning and development challenges, have access to and participate in the general school system"* (Mahlo, 2011, p.15).

Inclusion has its roots in special education as it is known today. Special education sector growth has included a number of stages in which education systems have discussed various ways of relating to children with disabilities and to students with learning difficulties (Sudha Samir Pingle & Indu Garg, 2015).

Inclusion is a process of responding to the diversity of needs among all learners, through increasing participation in learning, cultures, and communities, and reducing exclusion from and within education (Hazel and David, 2010). It involves changes in content, approaches, structures, and strategies, driven by a common vision that covers all children and the conviction that it is the responsibility of the regular system to educate all of them. These include:-

- Inclusion is about defining and removing barriers: therefore, gathering, collecting and evaluating information from a wide variety of sources to plan for policy and practice changes. It's about using all kinds of evidence to improve creativity and problem solving.
- Inclusion is about the presence, participation and achievement of all students: 'presence' is about where children are educated and how reliably they attend; 'participation' is about the quality of their experiences while they are present and must incorporate the views of the learners themselves; 'achievement' is about learning outcomes throughout the curriculum, not just testing.
- Inclusion includes a particular focus on those groups of learners that may be at risk of marginalisation, exclusion

or under-realisation: this means that there is a social responsibility to ensure that those communities that are clinically most 'at risk' are carefully monitored and that steps are taken to ensure their inclusion, involvement and success in education where appropriate.

- Inclusion is a process: Inclusion must be seen as an endless search for better ways to respond to diversity. It's about learning about diversity how to understand differences. In this way, differences are viewed more positively as a motivation for both children and adults to foster learning.

E. **Inclusive School:** The terms 'full-service schools' and 'inclusive schools' are utilised traded in departmental documentation. The DBE conceives building the capacity of schools distinguished as full-service schools. The DBE portrays the concept as follows:-A full-service/inclusive school gets it those boundaries to learning are not as it were natural to learners, but can more over be social and systemic. Departmental documents, the words "full-service schools" and "inclusive schools" are used interchangeably. The DBE plans to build the capability of schools that are known as full-service schools. The DBE describes the definition as follows. A full-service / inclusive school understands that developmental challenges are not only fundamental to learners but can be cultural and systemic as well (Daniels & Gamer, 2013).

However, a number of widely held beliefs in education and school culture can seriously challenge this application process. It is far more than intellectually challenging to locate the concept of inclusive education as both an educational concept and a practical application. It is one of the most difficult tasks in the field of education of all academic pursuits. Because inclusive education is an exceptionally broad term that includes all individuals to one degree or another, efforts to define it require broad strokes and broad applications while maintaining very specific verbiage (Shyman, 2015).

2.4 Theoretical Review

Different models and viewpoints from specific disability and inclusive education experts will be explored and objectively examined under this subtitle. The theoretical implications of this research is the concepts of the social disabilities model (Oliver, 1990), the theory of the formation of human capital and the environment of inclusive education (Bronfenbrenner, 1989). Such ideas are selected to illustrate the condition and its associated implications if access to education is denied to these children.

According to Robert Osgood (2005) as cited, Dudley-Marling & Burns, (2014) observed in his History of Inclusion in the United States that a significant proportion of students with disabilities in the United States, especially students with intellectual disabilities, were considered uneducatable until relatively recently.

Similarly, (Hornby, 2015) explained that inclusive education is generally considered to be a multi-dimensional term that involves the recognition and appreciation of difference and inclusion, acknowledgement of human rights, social justice and equality concerns, as well as a social model of disabilities and a socio-political model of education.

2.4.1 Models of Disability

Children with disabilities, their families, and social workers offering services are faced with negotiating complex social, community systems for behavioural, economic, and day-to-day home assistance. The fashions with disorders offer conceptual frameworks for interpretation and action that can inform the choice-making system of parents and social workers to develop these individual and cultural environmental complexes. As provided by the presentation (Howgego, C., Miles, S., & Myers, 2014). Models are sets of guiding assumptions on disability handout models; human-made devices for information and suggestions for movement; permit recognition of the assets and causes of disability; which are the representations of truth; are best-invented human assumptions and, to some extent, are culture-bound and time-safe. There are five impairment models, according to him; religious / moral model, physiological model, practical model, environmental model, and socio-political version. The last three models are engaging with those fashions. No specific models thoroughly describe the experience of disability and all these models portray disabilities as one-dimensional. These are explained as follows:-

A. **Public Studies Model:-** This model subsumes different disciplines that are related to each other because the interaction between policy and people is essentially associated with each other. This was the most dominant way of thinking about disability in the United States during the Twentieth century, along with the Model of Human Capacity, particularly during the last 30 years. The key principles correlated with this paradigm include anti-discrimination, equality, independence, privacy and secrecy, diversity, contextual sensitivity, business management and cooperation, empowerment / participatory decision-making, capacity-building and recognition of individual and programme (Perdana, 2018).

B. **Model of Human Capacity Studies:-** It deals with human development studies in general; how people learn different capacities. This was also divided into three sub-models: medical / public health, social, and educational groups through which each one played and continues to play a major role in disability policies and care and thus in the effect core concepts and relationships have on the quality of life of the family (John Clarkson & Coleman, 2015).

C. **Ethical and Philosophical Model:-** This model deals with the principles and philosophies that form the concepts of Cultural Studies and Public Studies. Security from injury, security and change, flexibility, and cultural sensitivity are the central themes associated with this model (Gelond *et al,* 2018).

D. **Model of Cultural Studies:-** The model addresses disability and the role of the disabled person and family from the point of view of how they are viewed in their particular society. Cultural responsiveness distinction, social dignity and unity family emphasis, autonomy, independence, and harm protection are the main concepts associated with this model. Five sub-models are available: cultural anthropology, economics, literature performing arts, and models of history (Vos *et al*, 2016).

E. **Model of Technology Studies:-** This model issues the "built" or environment, the physical world in which people with disabilities and their family lives. Anti-discrimination, productivity, integration, appropriate and individualised services and capacity building are the key concepts associated with this model (Dwivedi, Y.K., Rana, N.P., Jeyaraj, A., Clement, M., & Wiliams, 2019). Al though a radical implementation of four models has characterised the worldwide experience of disability, including voluntary medical assistance and the human rights model, each of which is discussed briefly below:

- **Human Rights Model:-** The human rights model recognises disability as an essential aspect of human culture and affirms that all human beings have certain rights that are inalienable irrespective of their disabilities. This model is based on the principles of the 1948 Universal Declaration of Human Rights, which states that all human beings are born free and equal in rights and dignity (Degener, 2017).

- **Social Model of Disability:-** The social disability model is based on a distinction between the terms "disability" and "disability" with its fundamental equality aspect and strongly believes in the phrase "Nothing about us without us." The model addresses issues such as underestimating the potential of people with disabilities to contribute to society by improving economic values if equal rights, suitable facilities and opportunities are provided. Social model of disability conceptualises disability as arising from the interaction of a person's functional status with the physical, cultural, and policy environments (Klionsky, 2007).

- **Medical Model of Disability:-** This model supports the idea that a disabled person is a victim and has to be treated or cared for and defends the fact that people with disabilities are actively removed from society. The medical model/individual model of disability views people with a disability as having a deficiency or impairment that needs to be "fixed" (Anglae, 2012).

In addition this model looks at a person's impairment first and focuses on the impairment as the cause of disabled people being unable to access goods and services or being able to participate fully in society. Since scholars of this model of disability as they focus on the impairment and what a person is unable to do they planned on what can be done to 'fix' the disabled person or provide special services for them as an individual. Because of this believe on the model some scholars express it as it distorts people's perceptions of humanity and relationships between human individuals, and its influence in the oppression of all people, both disabled and non-disabled (Cameron, 2011).

- **Charity Model of Disability:-** This model treats disabled people / PWDs as helpless victims in need of 'care' and 'protection.' Disability was perceived as a disqualification in the core of this model to claim the right to social resources that ensured the exclusion of PWDs from social arrangements, public services, and justified their exclusion from mainstream education and employment (Phtiaka, 1999).

2.5 The Present Status of Implementing Inclusive Education

2.5.1 Practice of Inclusion

Inclusion is limited as several methods have been used by teachers and educational professionals that prove beneficial to students with special needs. When examining best inclusive practices we first need to look at what is required to develop a good inclusion programme Inclusion programmes should include a belief that all children have the potential to learn and develop, the ability to respond to the student's cultural and socio-economic needs, the ability to promote positive behaviour in and out of the classroom, a dedication to seeing each child as an adult, and curriculum and activity changes to include all students (Stouts, 2001).

2.5.2 The Practice of Inclusive Education in the World

According to WHO (2013) as conducted that, in average, 10%

of any population is disabled. With this assumption approximately 85% of the world's children with disability of the age below 15 years live in the developing countries). And this paper also reminded that the right to education for all children is preserved in the universal declaration of human rights. However, in developing countries, the proportion of disabled children attending school is estimated between less than 1% and 5%. As (UNESCO, 2015), indicated that, lack of data on people with disabilities is severely constraining the ability of the international community to monitor the situation of children, youths and adults with disabilities.

2.5.3 The Practice of Inclusive Education in the Africa

According to Srivastava, de Boer, & Pijl, (2015) as cited Inclusive education focused primarily on the position of special needs students. Such children are not even entering schools in many states, let alone a special one. In many legal treaties, the right of children with special needs to attend a regular school has its roots, the most recent being the UN Convention on the Rights of Persons with Disabilities (UNCRPD, 2006). However, this isn't always the case for the developing world. For instance: 57 million primary-age children are not attending school (UNESCO, 2011) and then the focus is more on providing EFA than making schools more inclusive. Due to the different contexts and backgrounds of the Western world compared to developing countries the same set of factors may not be applicable. Thus, it is possible that in developing countries other factors and actors play important roles. This is likely to result in differences in the pace of implementing inclusive education. A different pace of implementation is obvious in regions such as Africa, Asia, and Southeast Asia.

2.5.4 The Practice of Inclusive Education in Ethiopia

Ethiopia has designed and implemented various legal frameworks that can support the effectiveness of access and quality of inclusive education for children with disability. Even though Ethiopia has accepted various international conventions and policy instruments the participation rate of children with disabilities (CWDs) still insignificant and did not achieve the needs of children with disabilities as well as for those of with special talents (Sori *et al.,* 2016).

As forwarded in the paper, in Ethiopia special needs education has long suffered insufficient recognition and little understanding among government bodies at various levels, schools and the society at large. In addition, the findings showed that the existing inclusive education is not well organised and structured to provide equal access to education for students with disabilities/ special needs. Equal access to education is limited and it access is still low. As shown in ESDP four, the country planned to increase the enrolment of students with SNE from 47,461 in 2009/10 to 1,739,000 in 2014/15 (MoE, 2012).

Accordingly, in its ESDP five MoE, (2015), indicated that the exact number of disabled children in Ethiopia is unknown. Instead the WHO estimate rate is used for planning purposes, stating that the prevalence of disabled people in any population will 10 million.

2.6. The Role Government in Implementing Inclusive Education

2.6.1 Inclusive Education from Legislation Perspectives

It is important to adapt national policies and laws once a country has committed to the concept of inclusion in education. Children with disabilities education and the value of inclusive education are better incorporated into the overall strategic education plan of the government, with implementation approaches expressed in the policy implementation plan for national education. The commitment to inclusive education is therefore clearly reflected in the overall national agenda and strategic planning, included in the education budget, and recognised in bilateral and multi-lateral agreements with funding agencies (UNESCO, 2009).

A dominant problem in the disability field is lack of access to education for both children and adults with disabilities. Therefore, in order to improve this problem which is hindering the participation and beneficiary of 10 to 17 percent of the total population of the world from accessing social services like education many legislations, proclamations, agreements, policies and strategies were designed and signed both at universal, continental and country level in line with universal declaration of human rights. These legal frameworks encourage and support the implementation of inclusive education for disabled and other marginalised groups all over the countries. Thus, in this section I tried to assess the legal frameworks which were announced and signed both at universal and country/Ethiopia level to assist and to make effective the access and quality of inclusive education. So the detailed discussion in both cases is presented as follows.

2.6.2 Legal Frameworks Related to Inclusive Education at Universal Level

To make children with disability participant and included in the education system and other general rights it has taken a long time. But still the access and quality of inclusive education to children with disability has large problem all over the world. Therefore, the education service to deliver on the right of all children to have a quality education; the system need to respond to the needs of all children including children with disability. In recent years, frameworks have begun to articulate what a rights-based approach to educating disabled children might look like from this human rights perspective. The solution is rooted in the creation of an equitable system of education. And, generally traced back to the Declaration of Human Rights in 1948, the journey to inclusive education for disabled children (UNESCO, 2009).

2.6.3 Legal Frameworks Related to Inclusive Education at Ethiopia Level

A variety of rules, regulations, initiatives and expectations for people with disabilities, including their right to successful and fair jobs, have been adopted and implemented by the Government of Ethiopia (Fentahun, 2013). The main ones are listed below:

1. The National Disability Action Plan (2012-2021) aims to transform Ethiopia into an inclusive society. It discusses the need for adequate recovery services for people with disabilities in Ethiopia, equitable opportunities for education, skills training and work, as well as full participation in the lives of their families, communities and country.

2. Federal Democratic Republic of Ethiopia's constitution: it was adopted in 1995. Article 41(5) of the Constitution lays out

the duty of the State to provide the necessary care and support services for disabled people.

3. Developmental Social Welfare Policy (1997): The policy specifically addresses people with disabilities and aims at safeguarding their rights and facilitating vocational rehabilitation programmes.

4. The 2010-2015 Growth and Transformation Project (GTP) identifies disabilities as a cross-cutting growth area with an emphasis on disability awareness and education and training, rehabilitation and equal access and resources for people with disabilities.

5. The declaration provides for special priority, among other things in recruiting supporting and deploying qualified disabled candidates such provision applies only to the offices of the government.

6. The Federal Democratic Republic of Ethiopia's MOE designed and implemented the first special needs education programme strategy in 2006. The second and revised strategy aimed at '... constructing an inclusive education system that will provide quality, relevant and equitable education and training for all children, young people and adults with special needs for education and ultimately enable them to do so (Moe, 2012).

7. Labour Proclamation, No. 377/2003, revised by Labour Proclamation No. 494/2006, makes it illegal for an employer to discriminate against workers on the grounds of race, class, ethnicity, political outlook or on any other terms.

8. National Plan of Action for the Rehabilitation of Persons with Disabilities (1999): aims at implementing meaningful action on disability through encouraging community participation; empowering people with disabilities and promoting a better standard of living by capacity building; and ensuring equal rights and full participation in society.

9. Proclamation on the Concept of Powers of Responsibility of the Federal Democratic Republic of Ethiopia Executive Organs, No. 691/2010, establishes requirements for equal

opportunities and full participation of persons with disabilities and persons living with HIV / AIDS.

10. The Education and Training Policy / ETP (1994): notes that all children, including those with special needs for education, learn according to their full potential and needs.

11. Proclamation on Employee rights for Disabled People, No. 568/2008. This proclamation invalidates all statute, practice tradition, attitude and other discriminatory situations that restrict equal opportunities for disabled persons. It also requires employers to provide suitable facilities for work and training; take all appropriate accessibility steps and affirmative action, particularly when employing people with disabilities; and assign an assistant to allow a person with disabilities to do their work or pursue their training.

12. Construction Proclamation, No. 624/2009, provides in the construction and design of any construction for accessibility to ensure suitability for physically impaired persons.

2.6.4 Ethiopia Policies and Strategies on Disability

In 1994, the Ethiopian government developed a new strategy on education and training (ETP). According to this proposal, "expanding quality primary education for all people is not just a right, but also a growth guarantee". The programme seeks to provide education without discrimination to all children and ensures that additional assistance is provided to disadvantaged groups in school. To this effect, it states the provision of special education and training for disabled persons '(Educational Structure No.3.2.9). In one of its specific goals, the strategy has emphasised that attempts will be made to allow both the disabled and the skilled to develop according to their ability and need' (MoE, 1994). According to the government's proclamation No. 568/2008 on the employment rights of people with disabilities, a person with disabilities refers to an adult whose equal employment opportunities are limited as a result of physical, mental or sensory impairments by social, economic and cultural discrimination. The statute simply prohibits employees in government offices from recruiting, encouraging and distributing civil servant workers (Asefa, 2008).

2.6.5 Ethiopia Constitutional Rights

According to Meseret Assefa (2018) stated that, Disability is specifically referred to in Article 41 of the 1995 Constitution on Economic Social and Cultural Rights: The State shall allocate resources within available means to provide care and support to the physically and mentally disabled the elderly and children left without parents or guardians.

1. Article 41 of the Constitution also states that every citizen of Ethiopia has the right to equal access to publicly funded social services.
2. Article 25 on the right to equality does not include disabilities in its list of reasons for non-discrimination, including gender, race and so on.
3. Article 9.4 states that 'All international agreements ratified by Ethiopia are part of land law'.

2.6.6 Legal Framework's in Support of Inclusion 1948-2007

Ethiopia has approved and accepted various international convictions and policy tools relevant to special need education or inclusive education in order to implement legal frameworks in support of inclusion. From these 1948 Universal Declaration of Human Rights– for the first time in this declaration, a general right to education was expressed directly and specifically in line with Article 26(1) states that "Everyone has the right to education. Education must be free at least in the initial and fundamental levels. Elementary education is essential. Professional and technical education shall be made available in general, and higher education on the basis of merit shall be equally accessible to all. 1966 International Covenant on Environmental, Social and Cultural Rights 1975 Declarations on the Rights of Persons with Disabilities call for international and national actions to ensure the rights of persons with disabilities to all services, allowing them to develop their capacity and skills as far as possible and to accelerate their social integration process" (Meseret Assefa 2018).

2.7 Empirical Review

Many organisations and countries have designed and implemented so many legal frameworks across the world since 1948 to support inclusive education for disabled children. Despite these legal frameworks, the availability and quality of inclusive education for children with disabilities have passed through many issues and most of these children have not been enrolled and those who have been enrolled still drop out of school before the end of the school year due to many reasons. The state of the introduction of inclusive education for children with disabilities at both universal and Ethiopian level is therefore reviewed as follows.

2.8 Challenges facing to Implementing Inclusive Education

2.8.1 Challenges towards Inclusive Education

According to (MOLSA, 2010 and MoE, 2005), in Ethiopia, children with specific disabilities have not received any education and training that helps them to suit their needs due to their complex and diverse nature great support is needed from local government, NGOs and religious organisations to address their needs in the time programme. The following strategies are designed to provide an inclusive and integrated programme of education.

These are: the recent special needs / inclusive education programme strategy of the MoE, (2012) also points out that according to the revised education and training framework of 1994, regions and future levels are responsible for planning and implementing programmes for special needs.

Although the challenges of inclusive education within the Ethiopian education system may seem numerous, they are far from interesting. The Ministry of Education's special needs education strategy outlines a plan to move away from the situation of special schools described above, and develop a system in which disabled children can live in their home communities and attend neighbourhood schools (Franck, 2015).

However, as described in the ESDP Five (MoE, 2015) and ESDP Four (Hornby, 2015) reports, the key obstacles to comprehensive learning are lack of knowledge, expertise and dedication to integrating SNE support activities; lack of reliable information to identify the status of children with special needs and plan effective interventions; lack of a consistent management and administration structure; and inclusive education; poor school services, equipment and tailored teaching and learning resources for SNE in accordance with the absence of expectations and guidelines; insufficient pedagogical abilities of SNE educators; lack of a job framework to help teachers expected to work in integrated service centers and satellite schools; minimal understanding within the educational community. Based on UNESCO and other scholars stated the major barriers of inclusion as follows.

2.8.2 Barriers towards Inclusive Education

According to (Senge, 2000) conducted that, addresses this by saying that the school should include the parents and empower them to systematically identify their own challenges especially the challenges that could be in the way of optimal education for their children and to consider creative solutions that work for them. By doing so, the school becomes the parents and their children's tool. While implementing inclusive education in primary schools, teachers face many obstacles. Inclusive education is a course and therefore it is not possible to obtain this educational aim for all in a single day it takes several years.

Many classroom teachers lack confidence in their ability to build inclusive classrooms as they deal with special needs children and feel lack of experience in this area (Callan, 2013). Teachers must be able to work with a consultant to define suitable educational goals for the child in both academic and social areas.

In another hand (Butterworth, 2004) as conducted, there are many factors affecting the inclusion of children with disabilities in regular education. Such factors influence the success of equitable learning in both engagement and performance, suggested that the potential obstacles to the education of children with disabilities may be physical, social or economic. They also identified three basic obstacles to be included.

These incorporate social components (poverty and budgetary obstructions including direct, indirect, and opportunity costs of schooling; gender; biases, e.g., toward girls, children living with or influenced by HIV, children with disabilities, ethnic minorities; need of recognisable proof documents/birth certificate; relocation and portability; predominance of child labour on minors, in industry, or the casual economy; wellbeing and dietary status of children and struggle); division based factors (need of school instruction materials; legal and policy barriers; need of appropriate infrastructure for children with disabilities; quality of teaching and instructor preparing; the number of instructors per lesson; steady loss rates of instructors and non-teaching education staff; school safety, violence, sexual harassment, and corporal discipline) and infrastructural factors (need of transportation, distance to school, lack of water and sanitation at school; destitute condition of school offices; regular variables such as rains/flooding; Remoteness and need of rural development). Inclusive education is a course, and therefore it is not possible to achieve this educational goal for all in a single day it takes several years.

- **Attitudes**

The main barriers that society causes to inclusive education not particular individual impairments. Discrimination results in negative attitudes towards differences and can lead to a serious barrier to learning. Negative attitudes can take the form of social discrimination, lack of awareness, and traditional prejudices. With regard to disabled children, some recoveries still maintain established beliefs that there is no point in educating the disabled; often the problem is identified as being caused by the differences of the child rather than the short-coming education systems.

- **Parents and Community**

Without the active participation of parents as a wide range of community services, education for children with special needs cannot be achieved. If the community's beliefs and attitudes about the disability and children with disabilities are negative it improves the lives of families and makes life hopeless for children as well. A sample study by (Tirussew, 2005) on society's attitude towards disabled people in Ethiopia showed that most people have negative attitudes towards people with disabilities.

- **Teacher's Abilities and Competency**

The skills and attitudes of teachers can be major limitations for inclusive education. Staff training at all levels is often inadequate where training is available and often tends to be disjointed, uncoordinated and inadequate. Today, inclusive education creates new challenges in how teacher development is built and organised in a country through important training to meet special needs education in order to achieve the intended goals of inclusive education, various skills and training strategies are essential for special teachers to overcome system challenges.

- **Curriculum**

The curriculum is one of the biggest barriers or mechanisms in any educational system to promote the development of a more inclusive programme. Sometimes, a curriculum cannot address the needs of a wide range of different learners. The curriculum is centrally designed and rigid in many ways, allowing no flexibility to explore and experiment with new approaches for local adaptation or students. The material may be distant and therefore inaccessible and motivating from the world in which the students live. Inclusive curricula are based on a view of learning as something that occurs as students actively participate in making sense of their experiences.

- **Lack of School Physical Facilities**

Many learners, especially those with physical disabilities, are physically inaccessible to the vast majority of learning centers. The learning centers are often accessible in poorer, particularly rural areas, largely because buildings are run down or poorly maintained. For all learners, they are unhealthy and unsafe. Most schools are not designed to meet specific demands, and there is no international support from the government (UNESCO, 2003).

2.9 Conceptual Framework

A conceptual framework is used to make conceptual distinctions and organise ideas (Ravitch and Riggan, 2012).This section has defined and explained relevant concepts that are related to inclusive education such as disability, inclusion, inclusive education, inclusive school and barriers towards inclusive education.

Theoretical framework of practice and challenges of inclusive education.

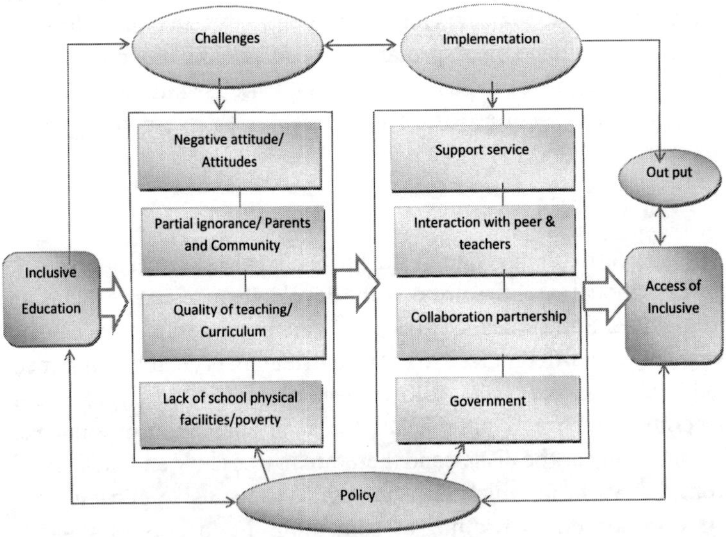

Source: Partial adapted from (Buntinx & Schalock, 2010).

Fig. 2.1: Theoretical framework of inclusive educational practice and challenges

Practice/Implementation; it's a driving force variable for IE (inclusive education) implementation. This includes government, parents, teachers and learners. To facilitate the implementation of IE, these partners need good cooperation. For the IE to be successful, each part of the operators has to play their role accordingly. The idea is supported by (Senge, 2000), who believes that the government will encourage teachers as the center of the process / operation. Government empowered teachers will be able to define curriculum' problems and possible solutions within and without the school community. In addition teachers will also participate in the introduction of IE as a center of parents / community involvement. Context, teachers, teaching and learning tools, supportive equipment, inclusive facilities and a learner-friendly environment (safety) are important to consider when introducing inclusive primary education. Inability to address these conditions resulting in poor implementation of inclusive education which is why more attention is paid to providing effective education for all learners in an integrated class. Inputs, there are many things to consider in order making inclusive education. (Msuya, 2005) suggests that, in order to ensure inclusive education, necessary facilities such as teaching and learning materials, equipment and some environmental settings are important for children with special needs. Hence the smooth running of inclusive education is very important to teaching skills, teaching and learning services, and government support. Even though, there are many challenges that tackle the implementation of inclusive education. These are negative attitude and partial ignorance of community such as parents and peer friends toward the students with disability, lack of school facility like conducive education environment, equipment, comfortable building and infrastructure to the student with disability and weak implementation of inclusive education curriculum. In general, policy is the important tools to implement the inclusive education in order to participate student with disability in education equally with healthy student and also it is necessary to overcome the challenges with legal framework.

Chapter Three

Research Methodology

3.1 Introduction

This chapter has includes:-Study Area Definition, Research Approach and Design, Population, Sample Size, Sampling Techniques, Data Collection System/Instruments, Data Collection Procedures, Data Analysis Method, and Ethical Consideration. This chapter was presented the research methods applied in line to answer the research question settled under chapter one. Based on this the chapter mainly concerned on how the research was conducted. Moreover, the chapter has shown and briefly presented the main and sub-parts of a research methodology which used to in the study including the research approach, the research design, data collection methods (source of data and data gathering tools), sample design (population, sampling technique, sample unit, unit of analysis and sample size) and data analysis techniques was used. Therefore, the detailed discussion was presented as follows.

3.2 Description of the Study Area

The study was aimed to assess the practices and challenges of inclusive education in primary school of Gambella Town Administration. The total population of the Gambella region design from 182,000 in 1994, to 307,000 in 2007, and to 409,000 in 2015, according to the Ethiopian Central Statistical Agency (2015). Over the years, this increasing population has put significant pressure on the land and its natural resources, including its forests and water (Chimdesa, 2017). In the western part of Ethiopia, Gambella is one of nine administrative regions. A total area of 25,521 km2 is covered by the region (M. Tadesse, 2007).

6° 28'38" North 8° 34' and 33° East Longitude 35° 11'11". It borders two other regions of Ethiopia, Oromia, to the north and east and Southern Nations, Nationalities, of People and the Regional (SNNPRS) to the south. It shares a South Sudan border to the west. The region consists of three administrative zones (Anyuak, Nuer and Majang) and 13 districts (woredas), one special woreda and one city government (UNICEF, 2016).

Gambella is one of Ethiopia's emerging regions. The economy is predominantly based on mixed farming among the people of Anyuak and Majang and agro-pastoral among the people of Nuer (M. Kottek, *et al.*, 2006). The region lacks connectivity among the districts (woredas) with poor transportation network.

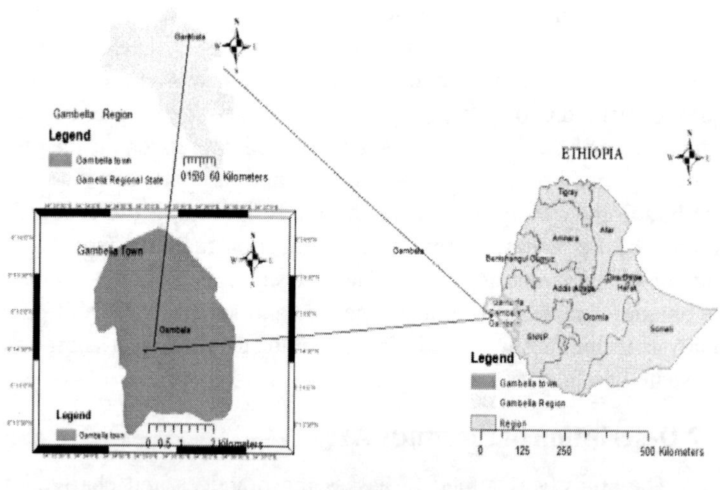

Fig. 3.1: Locational Map of the Study Area.

3.3 Research Approach

In this study a researcher used mixed research methods, both qualitative and quantitative. Because it is necessary in both approach to obtain relevant data through various data collection techniques. Since the purpose of this research used to assess the practices and challenges of inclusive education for children with disabilities, the study has been required to retrieve both quantitative and qualitative data from different sources and analyzing and interpreting it systematically using appropriate tools and techniques.

3.4 Research Design

According to Kothari (2004), the research design is important because it enables the smooth of the various research activities, so allowing research as efficient as possible generating maximum data with minimal effort, time and money expense. The experiment was used by exploratory research design. Because it is useful model ideal for the mixed research approach. To come up with a valid result in the study, triangular concurrent mixed method research design has been used, because, this method enables the researcher to cross-check the results and errors made using by quantitative method by qualitative method. Hence, here to comprehend the practices and challenges of inclusive education, a mixed method research approach used in lights with objectives of the study. Based on this, the researcher will use descriptive research design, in order to describe the current practices and challenges facing the implementation of IE for CWDs.

3.5 Research Method

This study uses both qualitative and quantitative methods of data collection. Quantitative data were gathered through, structural survey which is closed ended and open ended question. Key informant and in-depth interview, was employed to collect qualitative data in order to investigate and identify, practice and challenges of Inclusive Education on Primary school of the study area.

3.6 Population, Sample Size and Sampling Techniques

3.6.1. Population

The research used including targeted population as a participant or respondent in the field of study to obtain in-depth information on the issue in the area of study. The populations are inclusive education of primary school of a chosen Kebeles. The target population of this study were included the head of education office of Gambella Town Administration, special needs education expert, primary school cluster supervisors, 3 primary school principals, 81 primary school teachers and 687 students including with disabilities students who are enrolling in the academic year 2019 in all primary schools of the Gambella Town Administration.

Showing sampling techniques and samples which were selected from each population group.

Table 3.1: The Targeted Population

No.	*Participants selected*	*Sample selection technique/s used*	*Sample size*
1.	Total school principals selected	Randomly sampling	(8*263)/772≅3
2.	Total teachers selected including with disability teacher	Randomly sampling and purposive	(81*263)/772≅28
3.	Total students selected including with disability students	Randomly sampling and purposive sampling	(687*263)/772≅232
4.	Individual school principals	Purposive sampling	3 principals (1 each of the Schools)
5.	Individual teachers including with disability from each schools	Simple random sampling (lottery)	28
6.	Individual students from each schools including with disability	Simple random sampling (lottery)	232
7.	Disability students including with teacher	Purposive sampling	29 (which mean 24 students and 5 teachers)

3.6.2 Sample and Sample Size Determination

To get targeted sample size researcher used stratified sampling technique to determine the sample size of the study. The researcher use stratified sampling technique because of high population size which is difficult to manage data gathering from all population. So researcher was selected first three kebele randomly out of five kebeles which are 01, 02 and 04 kebeles. Then, from each kebele one primary school is selected randomly. Accordingly from 01 kebele, Dalcoch primary school, 02 kebele, Rasgobena primary school and Wuber primary school from 04 kebele was randomly chosen. After this, 37 students from grade seven, 35 from grade eight including with disability students and 9 teachers, 42 from grade seven, 47 from grade eight including with disability students and 11 teachers and 34 from grade seven, 37 from grade eight including with disability students and 8 teachers and 3 principals from the three schools above were picked from the list of population by lottery method respectively. Although, total number of student with disability of the three schools are 29 who were taken as respondents. Generally the sample size of the study will be 263 (Two hundred sixty three).

According to (Yamane, 1967) described that, to select the respondents a simplified equation for estimating sample sizes. As shown below, this equation was used for estimating the sample sizes. This formula used to calculate the sample sizes as shown below:

$$n = \frac{N}{1+N(e)^2}, \; N = 772$$

$$n = \frac{N}{1+N(e)^2} = \frac{772}{1+772(0.05)^2}$$

$$= 263.481229 \cong 263, \text{ so}$$

$$n = 263$$

Where n = Sample size and

N = target population

e = sampling error 5% or 0.05 at 95% confidence interval. According to the above computation the sample is determined as 263.

Table 3.2: The Sample size of the respondent showing sampling techniques and samples which were selected sample size

No.	*Name of schools*	*Sample size:- Grade 7,8, Principal and teachers of the school including with disability students*				
		G7	*G8*	*Teachers*	*Principal*	*Total*
1.	Dalcoch Primarily School	37	35	9	1	82
2.	Ras-gobena Primarily School	42	47	11	1	101
3.	Wuber Primarily School	34	37	8	1	80
Total		113	119	28	3	263

3.6.3 Sampling Techniques

Sampling techniques is the mechanism in which you choose from a larger population a number of individual cases. Depend upon this; researcher was selected participants through stratified sampling. In order to select participants from the study area, a researcher was selected 3 kebeles out of 5 from the Gambella Town Administration by considering distance because of saving time and money. Inclusive education was chosen by systematic sampling of selected kebeles based on their schools, grade was selected from identified kebele through stratified sampling method, then select the respondent through simple random sampling techniques for the questionnaire as it used to give equal opportunities to respondents and to minimise bias and purposive sampling was employed to select participants for qualitative data, in order to collect relevant data on the issue.

The following diagram which shows the sampling techniques of the respondents:

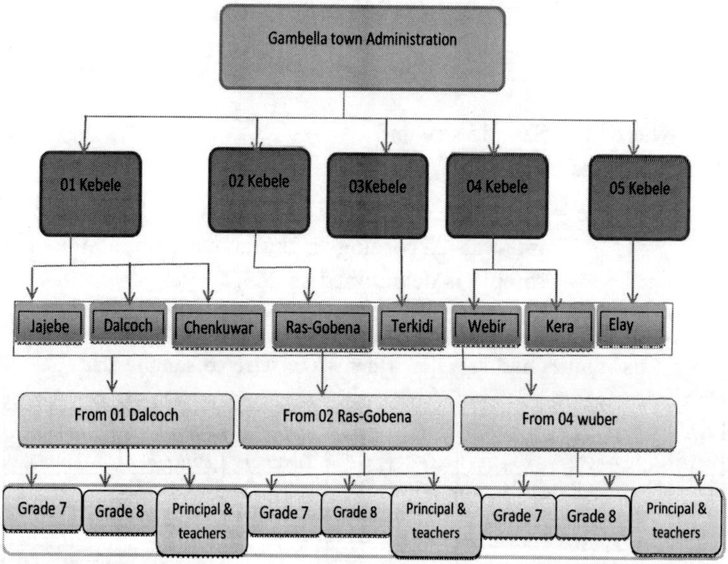

Source: Own field survey (2019).

Fig. 3.2: Distribution of sample taken from each strata.

3.7 Data Collection Instruments

According to Kothari, (2004), when doing research uses various types of data collection tools. As a result, a researcher must carefully use data collection instruments for his study in the research. Quantitative information was collected through a formal Questionnaire that is accessible and usable, while checklists will be employed to obtain data from key informant and interview guide questions was used to collect data from interviewee. In order to get detailed and deep insight responses to questions related with the present status of the implementation of inclusive education for students with disability.

3.8 Method of Data Collection

The study area researcher used his own technical data collection methods to collect effectively reliable data. However, during in-depth interview with the respondents, the researcher should give information about the objective and purpose of the report, take personal notice and raise questions to them. On the other hand, Questionnaire was modified through a time. Additionally, data gathered from selected respondents were carefully recorded in each day and dignity of the respondents must be kept in all level of data collection.

3.9 Methods of Data Analysis

Both qualitative and quantitative data were edited and coded after that the data were entered with the help of Statistical Package for Social Science (SPSS) to be ready for analysis. Then for quantitative data analysis, the descriptive method of data analysis was employed with the help of Statistical Package for Social Science (SPSS) version 25 to generate descriptive statistical results, which were presented using tables, graphs, and charts with the help of Excel and SPSS. According to Kothari, (2004), data to be transformed into a proper analyzable format, it must pass through a process of editing, coding, classification, and tabulation. The qualitative data obtained was carefully analyzed thematically to triangulate quantitative data and discussed.

3.10 Ethical Consideration

According to Leavy, (2017), for this part of research design, there are two main ethical issues. First, during the development of your research topic, ethical considerations emerge. Firstly, you were understand shielding the participants in the experiment and obtain the requisite permissions before you can start working with human subjects. A researcher was follow ethical consideration in all their work on the project based on this notion. First, the Department approves the title of the issue from the submitted topic. After that, accessible data sources that are applicable to the analysis were written in the right quotation, quote and link. Letters of permission from the University was asked for the collection of primary data from the study area. Participants must involve in the study based on their feelings and opinions were viewed as is their answer. Researcher was politely asked participants to engage in the study and make them aware of the study's purpose.

Chapter - 4

Data Presentation, Analysis and Interpretation

4.1 Introduction

This chapter presented and analyzed the data collected to seek an appropriate answer for the basic questions raised under chapter one of this study. The data have been presented, analyzed and interpreted thematically based on the research questions designed in chapter one. Therefore, the quantitative and qualitative data gathered using the above tools was analyzed and interpreted concurrently and consistently. The output was processed using the SPSS version 25 to get frequencies, percentage, and correlation. Thus, this section presents the results of the primary data collection tools questioner and interview. The results were arranged in line with the research question, literatures review and logically constructed questionnaires. The results were presented in tables, Statistical descriptive such as graph, pi-chart and table for each question and followed by narrative explanations by supporting the explanation with interview results as well as necessary secondary data triangulation has been made to support the explanation. Generally, this chapter classified into two parts. The first part deals with presentation, analysis and interpretation of data concerned on the characteristics and background of the respondents involved in the study in terms of sex, age, respondent status, type of disability and their religion. The second part has presented the presentation, analysis and interpretation of data concerning the practices and challenges of inclusive education in primary schools the case of Gambella Town Administration.

4.2. Data Presentation, Analysis and Interpretation of Background of theRespondents

4.2.1 Response rate

In this section the number of respondents which were planned and involved in both questionnaire and interview have been analyzed, presented and interpreted as follows.

Table 4.1: Table showing the response rate of respondents participated in questionnaire

Type of respondent	*Planned*	*Participated*		*Retrieved*	
		In number	*In %*	*In number*	*In %*
School principals	3	3	100	3	100
Teachers including disabilities	28	28	100	26	92.85
Students including disabilities	232	232	100	219	94.39
Total	263	263	100	248	94.29

Source: Own field survey (2020).

As shown in the table above the researcher planned to participate and retrieve 263 respondents in questionnaire. However, only 248 (94.29%) respondents replied the questionnaire distributed. Therefore, the response rate was above 90% which was good in getting the information needed for the study.

Table 4.2: Table showing the response rate of respondents participated in key informant

Type of respondent	*Planned*	*Participated*	
		In number	*In %*
Head of Gambella Town education office	1	1	100
Special needs education expert	1	1	100
Cluster supervisors	1	1	100
Planner education office	1	1	100
Total	4	4	100

Source: Own field survey (2020).

As indicated in the above table it was planned to made interview with 4 key stakes and informants concerning practices and challenges of inclusive education. Based on that, the researcher made key informants with 4 (100%) respondents which were sufficient to retrieve the information necessary for the study.

4.2 Background Characteristics of Respondents

This section presents and discusses the background of respondents in terms of sex, age, respondent status, types of there disabilities and their religion for better understanding of their situation. Accordingly, tables and figures present the background of respondents participated in this study.

A. Sex of respondents

Table 4.3: Table showing the sex of response

	Frequency	*Percent*
Male	154	59.5
Female	94	36.3
Total	248	95.8

Source: Own field survey (2020).

As the Table 4.3 shown; 154 (59.5%) were male and 94 (36.3%) were female. This showed that even if the study included both females and males majority of the respondents were males compared with females and this indicated that there is high number of male students and teachers than female students and teachers in the Gambella Town and this showed that there is a problem on equality among the number of male and female students and teachers in the town.

B. Age of respondents

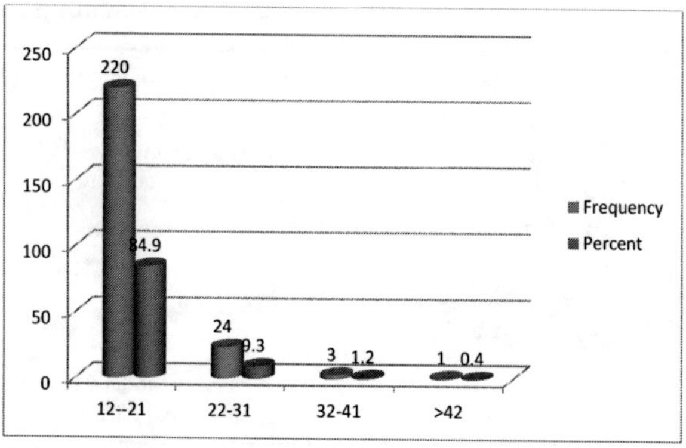

Source: Own field survey (2020).

Fig. 4.1: Ages of the Respondents

As indicated in the Fig. 4.1 above, the age of respondents ranges from 12 upto > 41 years age of respondents; 220 (84.9%) of them were between 12-21 age, 24 (9.3%) of them were between 22-31 age, 3 (1.2%) of them were between 32-41 age, and 1 (0.4%) of them were greater than 42 age. This shows that majority or 223 (86.1%) of the respondents were below/ under 21 age are students this is shown that the students are join their school in correct age of the school.

C. Respondent Status

Table 4.4: Table showing Respondent Status

	Frequency	*Percent*
Student	221	85.3
teacher	27	10.4
Total	248	95.8

Source: Own field survey (2020).

The Table 4.4 shows; 221(85.3%) of the respondents were students including with disability and 27(10.4%) of them were teachers including with disability. This shows that most of the respondents which were included in the study were students including with disability students. This implies that the researcher would able to get the necessary information needed for the study, because of their closure to the issue going to studied.

D. Type of disability of respondents

The following graph shows the type of respondent disability.

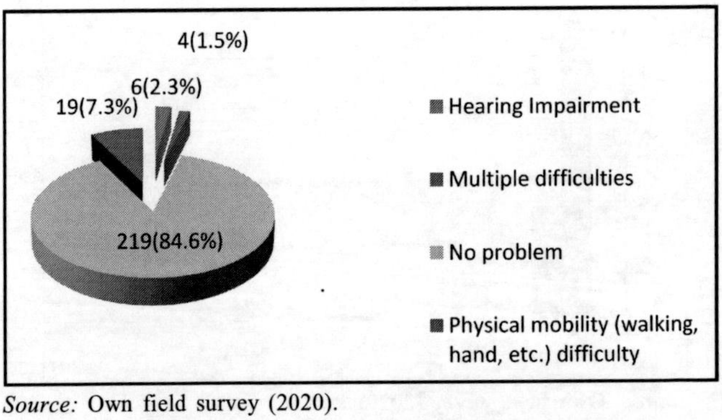

Source: Own field survey (2020).

Fig. 4.2: A Graph Showing Type of Disability of Respondents

The Fig. 4.2 illustrate; 6(2.3%) of them have hearing impairment, 4(1.5%) of them have multiple difficulties, 19(7.3%) of them have physical mobility (walking, hand, etc.) difficulty and 219 (84.6%) of them have no problem. This shows that the respondents have different disability. Therefore, the data gathered from this varied group helped to get necessary, sufficient and accurate information for the study concerned on challenges in implementing inclusive education both in access and quality.

E. Religion of respondents

Table 4.5: Table showingreligion of respondents

	Frequency	*Percent*
Orthodox	65	25.1
Muslim	60	23.2
Protestant	105	40.5
Catholic	18	6.9
Total	248	95.8

Source: Own field survey (2020).

The Table 4.5 shows that; 65 (25.1%) of them were orthodox, 60(23.2%) of them were Muslim, 105 (40.5%) of them were Protestant and 18(6.9%) of them were Catholic. This shows that the respondents have different religion. The majority of the respondents were protestant. This showed that there is no problem on religion among the religions of the students and teachers in the town.

4.3 Data Presentation, Analysis and Interpretation of Practices and Challenges of Inclusive Education

In this section, data concerning the present status of the implementation of IE, the roles of local government in the implementation of IE, challenges facing IE were presented by tables and figures, analyzed and interpreted thematically in order.

4.3.1 The Present Implementation Status of Inclusive Education

Inclusion is limited as several methods have been used by teachers and educational professionals that prove beneficial to students with special needs. When examining best inclusive practices we first need to look at what is required to develop a good inclusion programme Inclusion programmes should include a belief that all children have the potential to learn and develop, the ability to respond to the student's cultural and socio-economic needs, the ability to promote positive behaviour in and out of the classroom, a dedication to seeing each child as an adult, and curriculum and activity changes to include all students (Stouts, 2001).

Under this the issues related with Students are scored good result due to inclusive education. Education is accessible to all students with disabilities, the school gives awareness to the community about inclusive education. Students have equal access to education; including students with disabilities, strengthening partnership among stake holders, the school is well organised with school materials to implement comprehensive education the implementation of IE were analyzed, presented and interpreted.

1. The school gives awareness to the community about inclusive education

The following table shows the response on question concerned on the school gives awareness to the community about inclusive education.

Table 4.6: Table Showing the School gives Awareness to the Community about Inclusive Education

	Frequency	*Percent*
Yes	132	53.2
No	79	31.9
I don't know	37	14.9
Total	248	100.0

Source: Own field survey (2020).

As the Table 4.6 shows that; 79 (31.85%) of the respondents said that the schools were not implement the school gives awareness to the community about inclusive education, 132(53.22%) of them replied that the schools were work the school gives awareness to the community about inclusive education and 37(14.91%) of them said that they don't know whether the schools implement the school gives awareness to the community about inclusive education or not.

This shows most of the schools worked the school gives awareness to the community about inclusive education. In the same way the interviewees reflected that mainly teachers created awareness for parents and community regularly. However, still the community have awareness gap concerning disability.

2. Special need teacher's competency in treating students with disabilities

The following graph shows the Special need teacher's competency in treating students with disabilities.

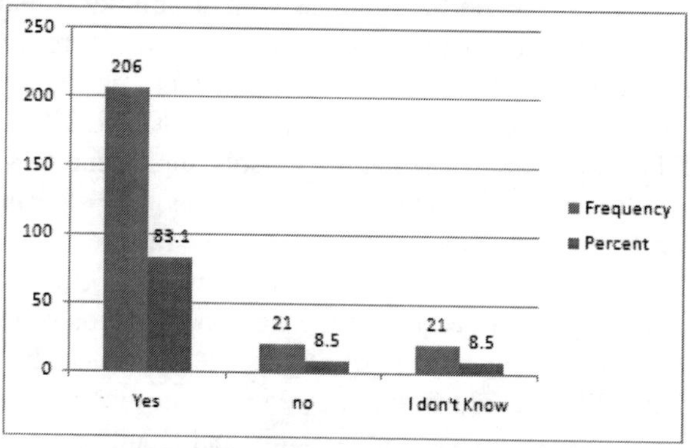

Source: Own field survey (2020)

Fig. 4.3: A Graph Showing Special need Teacher's Competency in Treating Students with Disabilities

As the Fig. 4.3 indicates; 21(8.5%) of the respondents said that the schools were not implemented Special need teacher's competency in treating students with disabilities, 206(83.07%) of them replied that the schools were work /exercise. Special need teacher's competency in treating students with disabilities and 21(8.5%) of them said that they don't know whether the schools implement the Special need teacher's competency in treating students with disabilities. This shows most of the schools worked Special need teacher's competency in treating students with disabilities.

3. The Woreda Education Office's role in empowering and supporting students with disabilities is minimal /poor.

Table 4.7: Showing the Woreda Education Office's Role in Empowering and Supporting Students with Disabilities is Minimal/poor

	Frequency	*Percent*
No	81	32.661
Yes	98	39.516
I don't know	69	27.822
Total	248	100.0

Source: Own field survey (2020).

The Table 4.7 shows; 81(32.661%) of the respondent said that the schools were not implement the Woreda Education Office's role in empowering and supporting students with disabilities is minimal / poor; 98 (39.516%) of them replied that the schools were work the Woreda Education Office's role in empowering and supporting students with disabilities is minimal /poor and 69(27.822%) of them said that they don't know whether the schools implement the Woreda Education Office's role in empowering and supporting students with disabilities is minimal /poor or not. In the same way the interviewees reflected that mainly the role in empowering and supporting students with disabilities is poor because of the woreda education offices has not given support and attention regarding disabled students. This shows most of the Woreda Education Office's role in empowering and supporting students with disabilities is minimal /poor.

4. Students are scored good result due to inclusive education.

Table 4.8: Table Showing Students are Scored Good Result Due to Inclusive Education

	Frequency	*Percent*
Strongly disagree	10	3.9
Disagree	6	2.3
Neutral	14	5.4
Agree	34	13.1
Strongly agree	184	71.0
Total	248	95.8

Source: Own field survey (2020).

As the Table 4.8 shows; most of the respondents strongly disagree 10(3.9%) replied, 6(2.3%) of them agree replied, 14 (5.4%)

of them neither agreed nor disagreed replied, 34 (13.1%) of them agreed replied and 184 (71.0%) of them strongly agreed replied. The majority 218(84.1%) of respondents agree, this shows that most of the respondents believe that the Students are scored good result due to inclusive education.

5. Special need education teachers are interested in teaching the students with disabilities.

Inclusion has its roots in special education as it is known today. Special education sector growth has included a number of stages in which education systems have discussed various ways of relating to children with disabilities and to students with learning difficulties (Sudha Samir Pingle & Indu Garg, 2015).

Table 4.9: Table Showing Special need Education Teachers are Interested in Teaching the Students with Disabilities

	Frequency	*Percent*
Strongly disagree	40	15.4
Disagree	30	11.6
Neutral	15	5.8
Agree	80	30.9
Strongly agree	83	32.0
Total	248	95.8

Source: Own field survey (2020)

As the Table 4.9 shows; 40(15.4%) of the respondents strongly disagreed, 30 (11.6%) of them disagreed, 15 (5.8%) of them neither agreed nor disagreed, 80 (30.9%) of them agreed and 83(32.0%) of them strongly agreed that the Special need education teachers are interested in teaching the students with disabilities. This reflects that majority 163(62.9%) of the respondents believe that Special need education teachers are interested in teaching the students with disabilities.

6. Education is accessible to all students with disabilities.

The Table 4.10 illustrates; 83(32.0%) of the respondents strongly disagreed, 29(11.2%) of them disagreed, 32(12.4%) of them neither agreed nor disagreed, 44(17.0%) of them agreed and 60(23.2%)

Table 4.10: Table Showing Education is Accessible to all Students with Disabilities

	Frequency	*Percent*
Strongly disagree	83	32.0
Disagree	29	11.2
Neutral	32	12.4
Agree	44	17.0
Strongly agree	60	23.2
Total	248	95.8

Source: Own field survey (2020).

of them strongly agreed that the Education is not accessible to all students with disabilities. This reflects that majority 112(43%) of the respondents believe that the Education is not accessible to all students with disabilities. Similarly, according to ESDP five MoE, (2015), indicated that the exact number of disabled children in Ethiopia is unknown. Instead the WHO estimate rate is used for planning purposes, stating that the prevalence of disabled people in any population will 10 million.

7. The school is well organised with school materials to implement comprehensive education.

Table 4.11: Table Showing the School is well Organised with School Materials to Implement Comprehensive Education

	Frequency	*Percent*
Strongly disagree	92	35.5
Disagree	58	22.4
Neutral	16	6.2
Agree	27	10.4
Strongly agree	55	21.2
Total	248	95.8

Source: Own field survey (2020)

As the Table 4.11 shows; 92(35. 5%) of the respondents strongly disagreed, 58(22.4%) of them disagreed, 16 (6.2%) of them neutral, 27(10.4%) of them agreed and 55(21.2%) of them strongly agreed that there was the school is not well organised with school materials to implement comprehensive education. This indicates that most 150(57.9%) of the respondents disagreed that there was the school is not well organised with school materials to implement comprehensive education. This in turn was influencing the effectiveness of both access and quality of IE.

8. Students have equal access to education, including students with disabilities

As forwarded in the paper, in Ethiopia special needs education has long suffered insufficient recognition and little understanding among government bodies at various levels, schools and the society at large. In addition, the findings showed that the existing inclusive education is not well organised and structured to provide equal access to education for students with disabilities/ special needs. Equal access to education is limited and it access is still low. As shown in ESDP four, the country planned to increase the enrolment of students with SNE from 47,461 in 2009/10 to 1,739,000 in 2014/15 (MoE, 2012).

Table 4.12: Table Showing the Students have Equal Access to Education, Including Students with Disabilities

	Frequency	*Percent*
Strongly disagree	20	7.7
Disagree	45	17.4
Neutral	35	13.5
Agree	49	18.9
Strongly agree	99	38.2
Total	248	95.8

Source: Own field survey (2020).

The Table 4.12 shows that; 20(7.7%) of the respondents strongly disagreed, 45(17.4%) of them disagreed, 35(13.5%) of them neither agreed nor disagreed, 49 (18.9%) of them agreed and 99 (38.2%) of them strongly agreed that the Students have equal access to education, including students with disabilities. This reflects that majority 148(57.1%) of the respondents believe that the Students have equal access to education, including students with disabilities.

4.4 The Roles of Local Government in Implementing Inclusive Education

The government has to play the greatest role to make the

implementation of inclusive education efficient and effective. In this regard the actual roles which were practiced by the local government of the town in supporting the implementation of inclusive education were discussed as follows. Based on this some of the teachers and school principals who were participated in questionnaire distinguished that the government have been implementing activities like the school principal gives sufficient administrative support to the student with disabilities through providing education stationary & supervising, creation of awareness about CWDs for the community, parents and children themselves; initiating and motivating parents in order to send their children to with disability to schools; Regularly school monitors and supervisors evaluate the implementation of activities designed to achieve inclusive education, collecting and transferring data concerning CWDs for bodies concerned; The roles of the Special Education Teacher in your school are paramount; supporting and monitoring the participation of CWDs in the education system and keeping record of data on CWDs. However, majority of the respondents both in questionnaire and interviewer organised that the government did nothing to support the implementation of activities of IE in schools.

1. The school principal gives sufficient administrative support to the student with disabilities through providing education stationary and supervising.

Table 4.13: Table Showing the School Principal gives Sufficient Administrative Support to the Student with Disabilities through Providing Education Stationary and Supervising

	Frequency	*Percent*
Strongly disagree	49	18.9
Disagree	37	14.3
Neutral	26	10.0
Agree	68	26.3
Strongly agree	68	26.3
Total	248	95.8

Source: Own field survey (2020).

The Table 4.13 shows that; 49(18.9%) of the respondents strongly disagreed, 37(14.3%) of them disagreed, 26(10%) of them neither agreed nor disagreed, 68 (26.3%) of them agreed and 68(26.3%) of them strongly agreed that the school gives awareness to the community about inclusive education. This reflects that majority of the respondents 136(52.6%) believe that the school principal gives sufficient administrative support to the student with disabilities through providing education stationary and supervising.

2. Woreda education office is give training and awareness to the students and school community about inclusive education.

Table 4.14: Table Showing Woreda Education Office to give Training and Awareness to the Students and School Community about Inclusive Education

	Frequency	*Percent*
Strongly disagree	47	18.1
Disagree	30	11.3
Neutral	30	11.3
Agree	62	23.9
Strongly agree	77	29.7
Total	248	95.8

Source: Own field survey (2020).

As the Rable 4.14 shows that; 47(18.1%) of the respondents strongly disagreed, 30 (11.3%) of them disagreed, 30(11.3%) of them neither agreed nor disagreed, 62 (23.9%) of them agreed and 77(29.7%) of them strongly agreed that the school gives awareness to the community about inclusive education. This reflects that majority of the respondents 139(53.6%) believe that the school gives training and awareness to the students and school community. This shows most of the schools worked awareness raising activities. In the same way the interviewees reflected that mainly teachers created awareness for parents and community regularly. However, still the community have awareness gap concerning-disability.

3. Regularly school monitors and supervisors evaluate the implementation of activities designed to achieve inclusive education.

The Table 4.15 shows that; 49(18.9%) of the respondents strongly disagreed, 37(14.3%) of them disagreed, 26(10%) of them neither agreed nor disagreed, 68 (26.3%) of them agreed and 68(26.3%)

Table 4.15: Table Showing Regularly School Monitors and Supervisors Evaluate the Implementation of Activities Designed to Achieve Inclusive Education

	Frequency	*Percent*
Strongly disagree	49	18.9
Disagree	37	14.3
Neutral	26	10.0
Agree	68	26.3
Strongly agree	68	26.3
Total	248	95.8

Source: Own field survey (2020).

of them strongly agreed thatregularly school monitors and supervisors evaluate the implementation of activities designed to achieve inclusive education. This reflects that majority of the respondents 136(52.6%) believe that regularly school monitors and supervisors evaluate the implementation of activities designed to achieve inclusive education.

4.5 The Main Challenges Facing to Implement Inclusive Education

In this sub-chapter the data concerned on Less commitment of parents to teach children with disabilities due to lack of awareness, Weak relationship among health students and students with disability, Parent's economic problem makes students with disabilities to do not attend in the school, school infrastructure, Support given to the students with disabilities by school principal is poor, Marginalisation of student disability by their peers and the community, Lack of self-confidence of student with disabilities, Abuse (suffering from psychological and/ or physical abuse) and Poor motivation students with disabilities for learning due to Environmental based factors which hindered the implementation of inclusive education were presented, analyzed and interpreted in brief below.

1. Less commitment of parents to teach children with disabilities due to lack of awareness

Table 4.16: Table Showing Less Commitment of Parents to Teach Children with Disabilities Due to Lack of Awareness

	Frequency	*Percent*
Strongly disagree	31	12.0
Disagree	34	13.1
Neutral	26	10.0
Agree	46	17.8
Strongly agree	111	42.9
Total	248	95.8

Source: Own field survey (2020).

The Table 4.16 illustrates that; 31(12.0%) of the respondents strongly disagreed, 34(13.1%) of them disagreed, 26(10.0%) of them neither agreed nor disagreed, 46 (17.8%) of them agreed and 111(42.9%) of them strongly agreed that less commitment of parents to teach children with disabilities due to lack of awareness. This reflects that majority 157(60.6%) of the respondents believe that less commitment of parents to teach children with disabilities due to lack of awareness.

2. Weak relationship among health students and students with disability.

Table 4.17: Table Showing Weak Relationship among Health Students and Students with Disability

	Frequency	*Percent*
Strongly disagree	27	10.4
Disagree	22	8.5
Neutral	22	8.5
Agree	73	28.2
Strongly agree	104	40.2
Total	248	95.8

Source: Own field survey (2020).

As the Table 4.17 shows that; 27(10.4%) of the respondents strongly disagreed, 22(8.5%) of them disagreed, 22(8.5%) of them neither agreed nor disagreed, 73 (28.2%) of them agreed and 104(40.2%) of them strongly agreed that weak relationship among health students and students with disability. The key informants further forwarded there is weak relationship among health students and students with disability due to lack of awareness. This reflects that majority 132(68.4%) of the respondents believe that there is weak relationship among health students and students with disability.

3. Parent's economic problem makes students with disabilities to do not attend in the school.

Table 4.18: Table Showing Parent's Economic Problem makes Students with Disabilities to do not Attend in the School

	Frequency	*Percent*
Strongly disagree	39	15.1
Disagree	27	10.4
Neutral	27	10.4
Agree	40	15.4
Strongly agree	115	44.4
Total	248	95.8

Source: Own field survey (2020).

As the Table 4.18 indicates that; 39(15.1%) of the respondents strongly disagreed, 27(10.4%) of them disagreed, 27(10.4%) of them neither agreed nor disagreed, 40 (15.4%) of them agreed and 115(44.4%) of them strongly agreed that the Parent's economic problem makes students with disabilities to do not attend in the school. This reflects that majority 155(59.8%) of the respondents believe that Parent's economic problem makes students with disabilities to do not attend in the school.

4. School infrastructures

Table 4.19: Table showing poorness of school infrastructures

	Frequency	*Percent*
Strongly disagree	10	3.9
Disagree	6	2.3
Neutral	14	5.4
Agree	34	13.1
Strongly agree	184	71.0
Total	248	95.8

Source: Own field survey (2020).

As the Table 4.19 indicates that; 10(3.9%) of the respondents strongly disagreed, 6 (2.3%) of them disagreed, 14(5.4%) of them neither agreed nor disagreed, 34(13.1%) of them agreed and 184(71.0%) of them strongly agreed that the existing school infrastructures were poorly fitted with the needs of CWDs. This shows that majority 218(84.1%) of the respondents believe that the roads, the school buildings, toilets, the water access and getes of the class rooms were poorly suited to the needs of CWDs. From this we can conclude that the school infrastructures are not conducive/ friendly to CWDs.

5. Support given to the students with disabilities by school principal is poor.

Table 4.20: Table Showing Support given to the Students with Disabilities by School Principal is Poor.

	Frequency	*Percent*
Strongly disagree	31	12.0
Disagree	71	27.4
Neutral	30	11.6
Agree	41	15.8
Strongly agree	75	29.0
Total	248	95.8

Source: Own field survey (2020).

As the Table 4.20 shows that; 31 (12.0%) of the respondents strongly disagreed, 71(27.4%) of them disagreed, 30(11.6%) of them neither agreed nor disagreed, 41 (15.8%) of them agreed and 75(29.0%) of them strongly agreed that the Support given to the students with disabilities by school principal is poor. This reflects that majority 116(44.8%) of the respondents believe that Support given to the students with disabilities by school principal is poor.

5. Marginalisation of student disability by their peers and the community

As the Table 4.21 shows that; most of the respondents strongly disagree 20 (7.7%) replied, 35(13.5%) of them agree replied, 31 (12.0%) of them neither agreed nor disagreed replied, 70 (27.27%) of them agreed replied and 92 (35.5%) of them strongly agreed replied.

Table 4.21: Table Showing Marginalisation of Student disability by their Peers and the Community

	Frequency	*Percent*
Strongly disagree	20	7.7
Disagree	35	13.5
Neutral	31	12.0
Agree	70	27.0
Strongly agree	92	35.5
Total	248	95.8

Source: Own field survey (2020).

This reflects that majority 162 (62.5%) of the respondents believe that the marginalisation of student disability by their peers and the community. However, the key informant interviewed reported that most of the time marginalisation of student disability by their peers and the community. This shows that the marginalisation of student disability by their peers and the community.

6. Lack of self-confidence of student with disabilities.

Table 4.22: Table showing lack of self-confidence of student with disabilities

	Frequency	*Percent*
Strongly disagree	39	15.1
Disagree	21	8.1
Neutral	31	12.0
Agree	38	14.7
Strongly agree	119	45.9
Total	248	95.8

Source: Own field survey (2020).

As the Table 4.22 indicates that; 39(15.1%) of the respondents strongly disagreed, 21(8.1%) of them disagreed, 31(12.0%) of them neither agreed nor disagreed, 38 (14.7%) of them agreed and 119 (45.9%) of them strongly agreed that the lack of self-confidence of student with disabilities. This reflects that majority 157(60.6%) of the respondents believe that lack of self-confidence of student with disabilities.

7. Abuse (suffering from psychological and/ or physical abuse)

Table 4.23: Table Showing abuse (Suffering from Psychological and/ or physical abuse)

	Frequency	*Percent*
Strongly disagree	33	12.7
Disagree	23	8.9
Neutral	30	11.6
Agree	49	18.9
Strongly agree	113	43.6
Total	248	95.8

Source: Own field survey (2020).

The Table 4.23 shows that; 33(12.7%) of the respondents strongly disagreed, 23(8.9%) of them disagreed, 30 (11.6%) of them neither agreed nor disagreed, 49 (18.9%) of them agreed and 113(43.6%) of them strongly agreed that the abuse (suffering from psychological and/ or physical abuse). This reflects that majority 162(62.5%) of the respondents believe that abuse (suffering from psychological and/ or physical abuse).

8. Poor motivation students with disabilities for learning due to Environmental, economic and social problems.

Table 4.24: Table Showing Poor Motivation Students with Disabilities for Learning due to Environmental, Economic and Social Problems

	Frequency	*Percent*
Strongly disagree	46	17.8
Disagree	23	8.9
Neutral	20	7.7
Agree	75	29.0
Strongly agree	84	32.4
Total	248	95.8

Source: Own field survey (2020)

As the Table 4.24 indicates that; 46(17.8%) of the respondents strongly disagreed, 23(8.9%) of them disagreed, 20(7.7%) of them neither agreed nor disagreed,75 (29.0%) of them agreed and 84(32.4%) of them strongly agreed that the Poor motivation students with disabilities for learning due to Environmental, economic and social problems. This reflects that majority 159(61.4%) of the respondents believe that Poor motivation students with disabilities for learning due to Environmental, economic and social problems. However, the key informant interviewed reported that there are lots of issues which include in the inclusive education program, but the only practice that we have been involving in facilitating a conducive environment for disable students.

Chapter Five

Summary, Conclusions and Recommendations

5.1 Introduction

This final chapter of the study presents a summary of major findings, concluding remarks and recommendations forwarded based on the finding of the study. In this, the first subsection describes a summary of the major findings; the next sub-section presents conclusions and the last subsection presents recommendations.

5.2 Summary

The purpose of this study was to investigate the challenges and the implementation of inclusive education in Gambella Town Administration. The researcher used school principal, cluster supervisor, IE expert, head of education office, teachers including special need regular teachers, students including with disability, questionnaire, and Woreda/ Town experts' interview, document analysis and observation to collect data. The participants of the study were 3 directors, 5 special need and 24 regular teachers, 232 students including with disability, Town head of education office, cluster supervisor and Town expert. For the purpose of investigation, the following research questions were formulated:

1. What is the practice of inclusive education for all students in study area?
2. What is the role of local government in implementing inclusive education in study area?

3. What are the challenges facing to implement inclusive education for all in study area?

In order to get answers for these research questions and to achieve the study objective, quantitative and qualitative data were gathered. The quantitative data were gathered from directors, teachers including special need regular teachers and student including with disability using questionnaire. The qualitative data were collected from experts through interview, focus group discussion and observation. Directors, special need regular teachers' questionnaire contains 27 questions that were designed to collect data about the required facilities to implement IE, the teaching learning process IE and challenges faced during implementation of IE. Moreover, observation was conducted to see inclusive education was carried out in accordance with the methods of IE and physical environment is conducive to implement IE. On the other hand, Woreda experts were interviewed to triangulate the information gathered through questionnaire.

The obtained data were analyzed with the help of SPSS. Such statistical tools percentages, frequency, were used to analyses the quantitative data whereas descriptive analysis was used for the qualitative part. Based on the analysis of the data, the researcher came up with the following major findings.

5.3 Discussion of the Major Findings of the Study

In this part, the findings of the questionnaire and the interview of the study were discussed and have been combined in a way that they supplement each other in the attempt made to assess the practices and challenges of IE in primary schools of Gambella town. The study generated several findings under each basic research questions. However, here in the discussion part only some fundamental issues have been taken and discussed based on the research questions and the purpose of the study. These issues are discussed under three major headings: the current status of the implementation of IE for CWDs; the roles of local government in the implementation of IE and the main challenges facing IE. Under and within the discussion of each major finding the researcher tried to compare and combine with the findings of the past studies conducted by different scholars.

5.3.1 The Current Implementation Status of IE for student including with disability

In identifying the current status of the implementation of IE for student including with disability the study examined issues like educational management and administration; educational access for CWDs; establishment of functional support systems for IE; conducting action researches and monitoring and evaluation of IE. In this regard the findings concerned on these basic issues have been discussed as follows.

Majority respondent responds that the schools worked the school gives awareness to the community about inclusive education. In the same way the interviewees reflected that mainly teachers created awareness for parents and community regularly. However, still the community have awareness gap concerning disability.

Concerning Special need teacher's competency in treating students with disabilities the majority respondents said that 206(83.07%) of them replied that the schools were work /exercise Special need teacher's competency in treating students with disabilities. This shows most of the schools worked Special need teacher's competency in treating students with disabilities. Regarding to Woreda Education Office's role in empowering and supporting students with disabilities is minimal /poor, 98(39.516%) schools were work the Woreda Education Office's role in empowering and supporting students with disabilities is minimal /poor and 81(32.661%) of the respondents said that the schools were not implement, the Woreda Education Office's role in empowering and supporting students with disabilities is minimal /poor. The rest 69(27.822%) of them said that they don't know whether the schools implement the Woreda Education Office's role in empowering and supporting students with disabilities is minimal / poor or not. In the same way the interviewees reflected that mainly the role in empowering and supporting students with disabilities is poor because of the woreda education offices has not given any support and attention regarding disabled students.

This shows most of the Woreda Education Office's role in empowering and supporting students with disabilities is minimal / poor. The majority respondents 218(84.1%) replied students\ are scored good result due to inclusive education. This shows that most of the respondents believe that the Students are scored good result due to inclusive education. The majority respondents 163 (62.9%) agree Special need education teachers are interested in teaching the students with disabilities. This reflects that majority of the respondents believe that Special need education teachers are interested in teaching the students with disabilities. The school is well organised with school materials to implement comprehensive education. Concerning increasing educational access to all CWDs most or 48.5% of the respondents reflected that the schools were implemented awareness raising activities on disability among parents and community at large, however, the gap is still manifested; 81.5% of them believed that the schools were not conducive to CWDs; 49.2% of them recognised that the schools were not provided necessary support to CWDs and with having these problems for the last two years (2016-2017) the average enrolment of CWDs in primary schools was 9.7% which indicates more than 90% of the children were not included in the education system but it exceeded the enrolment of CWDs 4.16% attended by the year 2018 at country level (MoE, 2018).

Regarding to Education is accessible to all students with disabilities the majority respondents 104(40.2%) was not agreed. This reflects that majority of the respondents believe that the Education is not accessible to all students with disabilities.

Regarding the issue of school is well organised with school materials to implement comprehensive education, most of the respondents strongly disagreed that there was the school is not well organised with school materials to implement comprehensive education. This in turn was influencing the effectiveness of both access and quality of IE. Concerning the Students have equal access to education, including students with disabilities, the respondents reflects that majority of the respondents believe that the Students have equal access to education, including students with disabilities. The school is well organised with school materials to implement comprehensive education.

5.3.2 The Roles of Local Government in Implementing Inclusive Education

Regarding the constitution of the Federal Democratic Republic of Ethiopia Article 41(5), the government at any level has are sponsibility that "the States shall, with in available means, allocated sources to provide rehabilitation and assistance to the physically and mentally disabled" (FDRE, 1995). Therefore, the local government (Zone, Woreda and Kebele) is required to implement this Article correctly.

The government has to play the greatest role to make the implementation of inclusive education efficient and effective. In this regard the actual roles which were practiced by the local government of the town in supporting the implementation of inclusive education were discussed as follows.

The school principal gives sufficient administrative support to the student with disabilities through providing education stationary and supervising. Concerning the school gives awareness to the community about inclusive education, 163(60.2%) of respondents agree this reflects that majority of the respondents believe that the school gives awareness to the community about inclusive education. The school is well organised with school materials to implement comprehensive education. Regarding regularly school monitors and supervisors evaluate the implementation of activities designed to achieve inclusive education, 136(52.6%) of respondents agree regularly school monitors and supervisors evaluate the implementation of activities designed to achieve inclusive education.

5.3.3 The Main Challenges Facing to Implement Inclusive Education

The main challenges that face to implement Inclusive Education in the study area, less commitment of parents to teach children with disabilities due to lack of awareness, weak relationship among health students and students with disability, parent's economic problem makes students with disabilities to do not attend in the school, school infrastructure, Support given to the students with disabilities by school principal is poor, marginalisation of student disability by their peers and the community, lack of self-confidence of student with disabilities, abuse (suffering from psychological and/ or physical abuse), poor motivation students with disabilities for learning due to Environmental, economic and social problems.

5.4 Conclusion

The main purpose of the study was to assess the practices and challenges of inclusive education to CWDs in primary schools of Gambella town. In this regard the researcher tried to examine the current status of the implementation of IE for CWDs; the roles of local government in the implementation of IE; the main challenges facing inclusive education that affect the implementation of IE. Therefore, by taking this into account and based on the discussions of the major findings of the study made, the following conclusions are drawn.The present implementation status of Inclusion Education, Inclusion is limited as several methods have been used by teachers and educational professionals that prove beneficial to students with special needs. The schools worked the school gives awareness to the community about inclusive education. In the same way the interviewees reflected that mainly teachers created awareness for parents and community regularly. However, still the community have awareness gap concerning disability. Special need teacher's competency in treating students with disabilities The Woreda Education Office's role in empowering and supporting students with disabilities is minimal/poor. In the same way the interviewees reflected that mainly the role in empowering and supporting students with disabilities is poor because of the woreda education offices has not given support and attention regarding disabled students. Regarding result of student and interest of teaching disable students, students are scored good result due to inclusive education and Special need education teachers are interested in teaching the students with disabilities.

However, inclusion has its roots in special education as it is known today. Special education sector growth has included a number of stages in which education systems have discussed various ways of relating to children with disabilities and to students with learning difficulties (Sudha Samir Pingle & Indu Garg, 2015). Similarly, teachers have not got any training regarding to disable students. Education is not accessible to all students with disabilities. Similarly, according to ESDP five MoE, (2015), indicated that the exact number of disabled children in Ethiopia is unknown. Instead the WHO estimate rate is used for planning purposes, stating that the prevalence of disabled people in any population will 10 million. The school is not well organised with school materials to implement comprehensive education. This in turn was influencing the effectiveness of both access and quality of IE. Students have equal access to education, including students with disabilities. As forwarded in the paper, in Ethiopia special needs education has long suffered insufficient recognition and little understanding among government bodies at various levels, schools and the society at large. In addition, the findings showed that the existing inclusive education is not well organised and structured to provide equal access to education for students with disabilities/ special needs. Equal access to education is limited and its access is still low. As shown in ESDP four, the country planned to increase the enrolment of students with SNE from 47,461 in 2009/10 to 1,739,000 in 2014/15 (MoE, 2012).

Concerning the roles of local government in implementing of IE, the government at any level is required to make sure that the Universal declarations and agreements signed by the country and other polices and strategies formulated by the state to support IE are changed into action. The government has to play the greatest role to make the implementation of inclusive education efficient and effective. In this regard the actual roles which were practiced by the local government of the town in supporting the implementation of inclusive education were as follows. Based on this some of the teachers and school principals who were participated in questionnaire distinguished that the government have been implementing activities like the school principal gives sufficient administrative support to the student with disabilities through providing education stationary and supervising, creation of awareness about CWDs for the community, parents and children themselves; initiating and motivating parents in order to send their children to with disability to schools; Regularly school monitors and supervisors evaluate the implementation of activities designed to achieve inclusive education. This shows most of the schools worked awareness raising activities. In the same way the interviewees reflected that mainly teachers created awareness for parents and community regularly. However, still the community have awareness gap concerning disability. However, majority of the respondents both in questionnaire and interviewer recognised that the government did nothing to support the implementation of activities of IE in schools.

Regarding the main challenges that face to implement Inclusive Education in the study area, less commitment of parents to teach children with disabilities due to lack of awareness, weak relationship among health students and students with disability, parent's economic problem makes students with disabilities to do not attend in the school, school infrastructure. Support given to the students with disabilities by school principal is poor, marginalisation of student disability by their peers and the community, lack of self-confidence of student with disabilities, abuse (suffering from psychological and/ or physical abuse), poor motivation students with disabilities for learning due to environmental, economic and social problems.

5.5 Recommendations

Based on the findings of this study, the study forwards the following recommendations: To overcome challenges facing the implementation of inclusive education and to improve both the access of education to those CWDs and quality of IE in the study area. To make the local government play their roles effectively initially the schools should organise and implement awareness creation activities like short term trainings discussions, panels, meetings and other strategies for political leaders and government bodies on disability and their role in the implementation of IE. Next to this the schools in collaboration with these political leaders and government bodies should work to raise awareness of parents and community at large concerning disability in deep. The Woreda educational office should modify the existing school infrastructures and facilities to fit with the needs of CWDs and making sure that the newly built infrastructures and constructed facilities have considered the needs of CWDs. Similarly, schools should establish IE resource centers in each cluster centers and schools possible by equipping with appropriate and sufficient resources and assigning skilled professionals on IE in each center.The government should work to establish special class rooms or schools at cluster center which are organised with appropriate and sufficient human and material resources through fund raising from different stakes including NGOs Schools should conduct action researches based on the problems they face while implementing activities of IE. Since this research was conducted only the practices and challenges of inclusion education, unlike this, there is a need to investigate which educational programme (integration and inclusive education) is more appropriate for Ethiopian primary schools. Therefore, future researchers need to investigate which educational programme is suited to the diverse needs of CWDs to implement in the existing incompatible situation of the schools in human and material resources, attitude, awareness, skill, curriculum, teaching approach etc they have.

References

- Ahsan. (2013). Inclusive education acts and policies in some selected countries including Bangladesh: A review. Bangladesh Education Journal, 5(1). 53-68.
- Alvarez. (1AD). SC-1, an antimycotic spirostan saponin from Solanum chrysotrichum. Planta medica, 67(04), 372-374.
- Anglae, K. (2012). Seasonal variation in kelp phlorotannins in relation to grazer abundance and environmental variables in the Alaskan sublittoral zone. Algae.
- Asefa. (2008). Combining ability of transitional highland maize inbred lines. East African Journal of Sciences, 2(1), 19-24.
- Bronfenbrenner. (1989). The developing ecology of human development: Paradigm lost or paradigm regained. Presented at the biennial meeting of the Society for Research in Child Development, Kansas City, MO.
- Buntinx, W. H. E., & Schalock, R. L. (2010). Models of Disability, Quality of Life, and Individualised Supports: Implications for Professional Practice in Intellectual Disability. Journal of Policy and Practice in Intellectual Disabilities, 7(4), 283-294. https://doi.org/10.1111/j.1741-1130.2010.00278.x
- Butterworth, D. (2004). Process heat transfer 2010. Applied Thermal Engineering. https://doi.org/10.1016/j.applthermaleng.2003.11.023
- Callan, L. (2013). A case study examining the inclusion of children with special educational needs in a mainstream primary school: A Case Study Examining the Inclusion of Children Louise Callan.
- Cameron, R. (2011). Mixed methods research: The five Ps framework. Electronic Journal of Business Research Methods.

- Chimdesa. G. (2017). The political economy of deforestation and forest degradation in Ethiopia: review article, J. Resour. Dev. Manag. 29 38-43.
- Daniels, H., & Gamer, P. (2013). Inclusive education. Inclusive Education, (February), 1-268. https://doi.org/10.4324/9780203062449
- Degener. (2017). A new human rights model of disability. In the United Nations convention on the rights of persons with disabilities. Springer, Cham. 41-59.
- Dudley-Marling, C., & Burns, M. B. (2014). Two perspectives on inclusion in the United States. Global Education Review, 1(1), 14-31.
- Dwivedi, Y.K., Rana, N.P., Jeyaraj, A., Clement, M.,&Wiliams, M. D. (2019). Re-examining the unified theory of acceptance and use of technology (UTAUT): Towards a revised theoretical model. Information Systems.
- Ehsaan, F., & Shahid, N. (2016). Inclusive education: A global Agenda. Journal of the College of Physicians and Surgeons Pakistan, 26(8), 726-726. https://doi.org/10.6033/tokkyou.41.613
- Engelbrecht, P. (2006). The implementation of inclusive education in South Africa after ten years of democracy. European Journal of Psychology of Education, 21(3):253-264. Available at http://download.springer.com/static/pdf/625 art%253A10.1007%252FBF03173414.pdf?auth66=13936883.
- Esther and Aluko. (2014). Challenges Facing Implementation of Inclusive Education in Public Primary Schools', Journal of Education and Practice, 5(16), pp.120-123.
- Federal Democratic Republic of Ethiopia. (1995). The Constitution of the Federal Democratic Republic of Ethiopia. Addis Ababa: The House of Federation of FDRE.
- Fentahun, M. (2013). Inclusion of People with Disabilities in Ethiopia. Available from: http://www.ilo.org/wcmsp5/groups/public/ed_emp/ifpskills/documents/publication wcms 112299.pdf [Accessed on 26 December 2016].

- Franck, B. (2015). Inclusive Education and Children with Disabilities in Ethiopia. 1-22. https://doi.org/10.1017/CBO9781107415324.004
- Gelond, M.L., Mishchuk, O.N. & Miroshina, E. (2018). Success as a philosophical category and a social phenomenon. Modern European Researches.
- Hazel, B. and David, C. (2010). Equity and Inclusion in Education; A guide to support education sector plan preparation, revision, and appraisal. Washington, DC 20433 MSN P6-600, 1818 H Street NW: EFA FTI Secretariat.
- Hornby. (2015). Inclusive special education: Development of a new theory for the education of children with special educational needs and disabilities. https://doi.org/10.1111/1467-8578.12101
- Howgego, C., Miles, S., & Myers, J. (2014). Inclusive Learning: Children with disabilities and difficulties in learning. Health and Education Advice and Resource Team, 22(7), 663-667.
- ILO. (2006). Implementing the global Employment Agenda: Employment Strategy in Support of decent work.Geneva 22, Switzerland: International Labor Office, CH-1211.
- John Clarkson, P., & Coleman, R. (2015). History of inclusive design in the UK. Applied Ergonomics, 46(PB), 235-247. https://doi.org/10.1016/j.apergo.2013.03.002
- Kassaw, A. (2017). Challenges and Opportunities in Inclusion of Students with Physical Disabilities in Physical Education Practical Classes in North Shewa Zone, Ethiopia. American Journal of Sports Science, 5(2), 7. https://doi.org/10.11648/j.ajss.20170502.11
- Klionsky, D. J. (2007). Autophagy: From phenomenology to molecular understanding in less than a decade. Nature Reviews Molecular Cell Biology. https://doi.org/10.1038/nrm2245
- Kothari, C. (2004). Research Methodology Methods and Techniques (Second). Retrieved from http://www.ghbook.ir/index. php?& option=com_ &task=readonline&book_id=13650&page=73&chkhashk=ED9 C9491B4&Itemid= 218&lang=fa&tmpl=component.

- Leavy. (2017). Qualitative,Quantitative, mixed method, Art-based, and community based participatory research approaches.
- M. Kottek, et al. (2006). World map of the Koppen-Geiger climate classification updated, Meteorol. Z. 15 (3) 259-263.
- M. Tadesse. (2007). Gambella the Impact of Local Conflict on Regional Security, Institute for Security Studies (ISS), Addis Ababa.
- Mahlo. (2011). Experiences of learning support teachers in the foundation phase with reference to the implementation of inclusive education in Gauteng (Doctoral dissertation).
- Matlala, M. (2015). Teacher support in the inclusive primary school: addressing barriers to learning in the classroom. https://doi.org/10.1145/3132847.3132886
- McLaren. (2013). Is inclusive education right for every child? An account by the parent of a child with high and complex needs due to autism spectrum disorder. Kairaranga,. 14(2), 26-34.
- Megan Walsh. (2017). Inclusion of Students with Special Needs in the General Education Classroom. https://doi.org/10.3926/ic.642
- Meseret Assefa. (2018). Implementation and Challenges of Inclusive Education in Harari Regional State in Selected Schools Addis Ababa, Ethiopia.
- MoE. (2018). Education Statistics 2016/2017. Addis Ababa, Ethiopia: Education.
- Mitiku, W., Alemu, Y., & Mengsitu, S. (2014). Challenges and Opportunities to Implement Inclusive Education. Asian Journal of Humanity, Art and Literature, 1(2), 118. https://doi.org/10.15590/ajhal/2014/v1i2/54051.
- MoE. (1994). Development of a new theory for the education of children with special educational needs and disabilities.
- MoE. (2015). Ministry of Education of Federal Democratic Republic of Ethiopia (2015) Education Sector Development Program V (ESDP V) from 2015/16 - 2019/20: Program Action Plan.Addis Ababa, Ethiopia: Federal Ministry of Education.
- Moe, H. (2012). Who participates and how? Twitter as an arena

for public debate about the data retention directive in Norway. International Journal of Communication.

- MOlSA. (2010). Disabilities and the influence of the African decade pronouncement in Ethiopia. "Rational for and benefits of inclusion" (2004), Retrieved June 14, 2004 from the world wide web:htte:www.palaestra.com/inclusion2.htm/.
- Msuya. (2005). An Assessment of PEDP Implementation, A case of Mara Region, University of Dar es Salaam.
- Murungi, L. N. (2015). Inclusive basic education in South Africa: Issues in its conceptualisation and implementation. Potchefstroom Electronic Law Journal. https://doi.org/10.4314/pelj.v18i1.07
- Oliver, M. (1990). The individual and social models of disability Joint Workshop of the Living Options Group and the Research Unit of the Royal College of Physicians on People with established locomotor disabilities in hospitals.
- Parekh, G. (2013). A Case for Inclusive Education. 1-41. https://doi.org/10.1136/bmj.311.7021.1691
- Perdana. (2018). Disability Definitions, Diagnoses, and practice Implications. Journal of Chemical Information and Modeling, 53(9), 1689-1699. https://doi.org/10.1017/CBO9781107415324.004
- Phtiaka. (1999). Disability, human rights and education in Cyprus. Disability, human rights and education: Cross-cultural perspective. 176-192.
- Pingle, D. S., & Garg, D. I. (2015). Effect of Inclusive Education Awareness Programme on Preservice Teachers (Vol. 151). https://doi.org/10.1145/3132847.3132886
- Ravitch and Riggan. (2012). Reason and Rigor: How Conceptual Frameworks guide Research, Thousand Oaks CA: Sage, p. 13.
- Reviews, P., Reports, C., & Parent, A. S. (2016). What Is an Education Savings. (June).
- Safford, K., Chamberlain, L., Donohue, D., & Bornman, J. (2018). The challenges of realising inclusive education in South Africa. Learning and Teaching Around The World, 34(2), 120-126. https://doi.org/10.4324/9780429491498-15

- Secretariat of the African Decade of Persons with Disabilities. (2010). Baseline Study on the Status of Persons with Disabilities and the Influence of the African Decade Pronouncement in Ethiopia: Policies & Program Implementation.
- Senge. (2000). Schools that learn. London: Nicholas Brealey.
- Shyman, E. (2015). Toward a Globally Sensitive Definition of Inclusive Education Based in Social Justice. International Journal of Disability, Development and Education, 62(4), 351-362. https://doi.org/10.1080/1034912X.2015.1025715
- Sikandar, A. (2017). Journal of Education and Educational Development. Journal of Education and Educational Development, 4(1), 32-47.
- Sori, D. A., Azale, A. W., & Gemeda, D. H. (2016). Characteristics and repair outcome of patients with Vesicovaginal fistula managed in Jimma University teaching Hospital, Ethiopia. BMC Urology, 16(1). https://doi.org/10.1186/s12894-016-0152-8
- Srivastava, M., de Boer, A., & Pijl, S. J. (2015). Inclusive education in developing countries: a closer look at its implementation in the last 10 years. Educational Review, 67(2), 179-195. https://doi.org/10.1080/00131911.2013.847061
- Stout. (2001). Jasmonate, mediated induced plant resistance affects a community of herbivores. Ecological Entomology, 26(3), 312-324.
- Sudha Samir Pingle & Indu Garg. (2015). Effect of Inclusive Education Awareness Programme on Preservice Teachers.
- Suleymanov, F. (2015). Issues of Inclusive Education: Some Aspects to be Considered. Electronic Journal for Inclusive Education, 3(4), 1-24.
- Tahir, Khazima Ed.D., Doelger, Brian Ed.D., and Hynes, M. E. D. (2019). A Case Study on the Ecology of Inclusive Education in the United States. Journal for Leadership and Instruction, (Spring), 17-24. Retrieved from https://files.eric.ed.gov/fulltext/EJ1222244.pdf
- Tirussew. (2005). Disability in Ethiopia: Issues, Insights and Implementation. Addis Ababa.

- Udoba, H. A. (2014). Challenges Faced by Teachers when Teaching Learners with Developmental Disability. Retrieved from https://www.duo.uio.no/bitstream/handle/10852/42438/Master-thesis-Humphrey-2-2.pdf?sequence=1
- UNCRPD. (2006). Convention on the rights of persons with disabilities.
- UNESCO. (2003). Open file on inclusive education: support materials for manager and administrators.
- UNESCO. (2009a). Policy guidelines on inclusion in education. Retrieved July 7, 2016, from http://unesdoc.unesco.org/ images/ 0017/001778/177849e.pdf.
- UNESCO. (2009b). Towards Inclusive Education for Children With Disabilities: A Guideline. Mom Luang Pin Malakul Centeral Building 920 Sukhumvit Road, Prakanong Bangkok 10110, Thailand: UNESCO Bangkok Asia Pacific Regional Bureau for Education.
- UNESCO. (2011). Recommendation on the historic urban landscape. In Records of the General Conference 36th Session. Paris: UNESCO.
- UNESCO. (2012). Addressing Exclusion in education: A guide to Assessing education Systems towards More inclusive and Just Societies. Available from: htto [Acc essed on 23 December 2016].
- UNESCO. (2015). El Crecimiento Insostenible Y La Creciente Demanda Mundial De Agua. In Wwdr.
- Unicef. (2017). Inclusive Inclusive. Inclusive Education, 1-8.
- UNICEF. (2016). Gambella Regional Briefing Note, UNICEF, Ethiopia.
- United Nations (UN). (1948). United Nations Universal Declaration of Human Rights 18. Available from:http://www.jus.uio.no/lm/ un.universal.declaration. of.human. rights.1948/portrait.a4. pdf [Accessed on 3 December 2016].
- University of Minnesota. (2019). Inclusive Education Strategies: A Textbook.

- Vos, T., Allen, C., Arora, M., Barber, R. M., Brown, A., Carter, A.,… Zuhlke, L. J. (2016). Global, regional, and national incidence, prevalence, and years lived with disability for 310 diseases and injuries, 1990-2015: a systematic analysis for the Global Burden of Disease Study 2015. The Lancet. https://doi.org/10.1016/S0140-6736(16)31678-6
- WHO. (1980). International Classification of Impairments, Disabilities, and Handicaps: A manual of classification relating to the consequences of disease. Available from: http://apps.who.int/iris/bitstream/10665/41003/1/9241541261_eng.pdf [Accessed on 23 December 2016.
- WHO. (2013). Disabilities, [Online], Available: http://www.who.int/topics/disabilities/en/ [18 Oct 2013].
- World Health Organisation (WHO). (2011). World report on disability. Retrieved October 6, 2016, from http:// www.who.int/disabilities/world_report/2011/en/.
- Yamane, T. (1967). Statistics, An Introductory Analysis, 2nd Ed., New York: Harper and Row.
- Zalalem Temesgen. (2014). The journey of special needs education, Bahirdar University, Ethiopia.

Index

O

P

Q

R

S